AMERICAN POLITICAL, ECONOMIC, AND SECURITY ISSUES

UNFUNDED MANDATES REFORM ACT: EXAMINING THE COSTS AND IMPACTS

American Political, Economic, and Security Issues

Additional books in this series can be found on Nova's website under the Series tab.

Additional E-books in this series can be found on Nova's website under the E-books tab.

Congressional Policies, Practices and Procedures

Additional books in this series can be found on Nova's website under the Series tab.

Additional E-books in this series can be found on Nova's website under the E-books tab.

AMERICAN POLITICAL, ECONOMIC, AND SECURITY ISSUES

UNFUNDED MANDATES REFORM ACT: EXAMINING THE COSTS AND IMPACTS

IRENE L. DE SILVA
EDITOR

Nova Science Publishers, Inc.
New York

For permission to use material from this book please contact us:
Telephone 631-231-7269; Fax 631-231-8175
Web Site: http://www.novapublishers.com

Additional color graphics may be available in the e-book version of this book.

Library of Congress Cataloging-in-Publication Data

Unfunded mandates reform act : examining the costs and impacts / editor,
Irene L. De Silva.
p. cm.
Includes index.
ISBN 978-1-61209-920-0 (hbk.)
1. Unfunded mandates--United States. 2. Unfunded mandates--Law and legislation--United States. I. De Silva, Irene L.
HJ275.5.U54 2011
336.3'90973--dc22
2011004965

Published by Nova Science Publishers, Inc. † New York

CONTENTS

Preface		**vii**
Chapter 1	Unfunded Mandates Reform Act: History, Impact and Issues *Robert Jay Dilger and Richard S. Beth*	**1**
Chapter 2	A Review of CBO's Activities in 2009 under the Unfunded Mandates Reform Act *Congressional Budget Office*	**65**
Chapter Sources		**137**
Index		**139**

PREFACE

The Unfunded Mandates Reform Act of 1995 (UMRA) culminated years of efforts by state and local government officials and various business interests to control, if not eliminate, the imposition of unfunded intergovernmental and private sector federal mandates. Advocates argued the statute was needed to forestall federal legislation and regulations that imposed obligations on state and local governments or businesses that resulted in higher costs and inefficiencies. Opponents argued that federal mandates may be necessary to achieve national objectives in areas where voluntary action by state and local governments and business failed to achieve desired results. This new book examines the debate over what constitutes an unfunded federal mandate and UMRA's implementation.

Chapter 1 - The Unfunded Mandates Reform Act of 1995 (UMRA) culminated years of effort by state and local government officials and various business interests to control, if not eliminate, the imposition of unfunded intergovernmental and private sector federal mandates. Advocates argued the statute was needed to forestall federal legislation and regulations that imposed obligations on state and local governments or businesses that resulted in higher costs and inefficiencies. Opponents argued that federal mandates may be necessary to achieve national objectives in areas where voluntary action by state and local governments and business failed to achieve desired results.

Chapter 2 - The federal government—through laws and regulations—sometimes requires state, local, and tribal governments and various entities in the private sector to expend resources to achieve national goals. In 1995, the Congress passed and the President signed the Unfunded Mandates Reform Act (UMRA) to ensure that, during the legislative process, the Congress receives information about such proposed requirements, known as federal mandates, before enacting a piece of legislation.

In: Unfunded Mandates Reform Act
Editor: Irene L. DeSilva
ISBN: 978-1-61209-920-0

Chapter 1

UNFUNDED MANDATES REFORM ACT: HISTORY, IMPACT AND ISSUES

Robert Jay Dilger[1] and Richard S. Beth[2]
[1]American National Government
[2]Congress and the Legislative Process

SUMMARY

The Unfunded Mandates Reform Act of 1995 (UMRA) culminated years of effort by state and local government officials and various business interests to control, if not eliminate, the imposition of unfunded intergovernmental and private sector federal mandates. Advocates argued the statute was needed to forestall federal legislation and regulations that imposed obligations on state and local governments or businesses that resulted in higher costs and inefficiencies. Opponents argued that federal mandates may be necessary to achieve national objectives in areas where voluntary action by state and local governments and business failed to achieve desired results.

UMRA provides a framework for the Congressional Budget Office (CBO) to estimate the direct costs of mandates in legislative proposals to state and local governments and to the private sector, and for issuing agencies to estimate the direct costs of mandates in proposed regulations to regulated entities. Aside from these informational requirements, UMRA controls the imposition of mandates only through a procedural mechanism allowing

Congress to decline to consider unfunded intergovernmental mandates in proposed legislation if they are estimated to cost more than specified threshold amounts. UMRA applies to any provision in legislation, statute, or regulation that would impose an enforceable duty upon state and local governments or the private sector. It does not apply to conditions of federal assistance; duties stemming from participation in voluntary federal programs; rules issued by independent regulatory agencies; rules issued without a general notice of proposed rulemaking; and rules and legislative provisions that cover individual constitutional rights, discrimination, emergency assistance, grant accounting and auditing procedures, national security, treaty obligations, and certain elements of Social Security.

State and local government officials argue that UMRA has restrained the growth of unfunded federal mandates, but that its coverage should be broadened, with special consideration given to including conditions of federal financial assistance. Reflecting these views, on May 5, 2009, Representative Virginia Foxx introduced legislation, H.R. 2255, that would, among other things, broaden UMRA's coverage to include assessments of the costs of conditions of federal financial assistance and reasonably foreseeable indirect costs. Also, on July 22, 2010, Representative Scott Garrett introduced legislation, H.R. 5818, to make private sector mandates subject to a point of order. Other organizations have argued that UMRA's coverage should be maintained or reinforced by adding exclusions for mandates regarding public health, safety, workers' rights, environmental protection, and the disabled.

This report examines debates over what constitutes an unfunded federal mandate and UMRA's implementation. It focuses on UMRA's requirement that CBO issue written cost estimate statements for federal mandates in legislation, its procedures for raising points of order in the House and Senate concerning unfunded federal mandates in legislation, and its requirement that federal agencies prepare written cost estimate statements for federal mandates in rules. It also assesses UMRA's impact on federal mandates and arguments concerning UMRA's future, focusing on UMRA's definitions, exclusions, and exceptions which currently exempt many federal actions with potentially significant financial impacts on nonfederal entities. An examination of the rise of unfunded federal mandates as a national issue and a summary of UMRA's legislative history are provided in an **Appendix**.

AN OVERVIEW OF UMRA, ITS ORIGINS, AND PROVISIONS

Overview

The Unfunded Mandates Reform Act of 1995 (UMRA) established requirements for enacting certain legislation and issuing certain regulations that would impose enforceable duties on state, local, or tribal governments or on the private sector.[1] UMRA refers to obligations imposed by such legislation and regulations as "mandates" (either "intergovernmental" or "private sector," depending on the entities affected). The direct cost to affected entities of meeting these obligations are referred to as "mandate costs," and when the federal government does not provide funding to cover these costs, the mandate is termed "unfunded."

UMRA incorporates numerous definitions, exclusions, and exceptions that specify what forms and types of mandates are subject to its requirements, termed "covered mandates." Covered mandates do not include many federal actions with potentially significant financial impacts on nonfederal entities. This chapter's primary purpose is to describe the kinds of legislative and regulatory provisions that are subject to UMRA's requirements, and, on this basis, to assess UMRA's impact on federal mandates. The report also examines debates that occurred, both before and since UMRA's enactment, concerning what kinds of provisions UMRA ought to cover, and considers the implications of experience under UMRA for possible future revisions of its scope of coverage.

This chapter also describes the requirements UMRA imposes on congressional and agency actions to establish covered mandates. For most legislation and regulations covered by UMRA, these requirements are only informational. For reported legislation that would impose covered mandates on the intergovernmental or private sectors, UMRA requires the Congressional Budget Office (CBO) to provide an estimate of mandate costs. Similarly, for regulations that would impose covered mandates on the intergovernmental or private sectors, UMRA requires that the issuing agency provide an estimate of mandate costs (although the specifics of the estimates required for legislation and for regulations differ somewhat). Also, solely for legislation that would impose covered intergovernmental mandates, UMRA establishes a point of order in each house of Congress through which the chamber can decline to consider the legislation. This chapter examines UMRA's implementation, focusing on the respective requirements for mandate cost estimates on legislation and regulations, and on the point of order procedure for legislation proposing unfunded intergovernmental mandates.

Origin

The concept of unfunded mandates rose to national prominence during the 1970s and 1 980s primarily through the response of state and local government officials to changes in the nature of federal intergovernmental grant-in-aid programs and to regulations affecting state and local governments. Before then, the federal government had traditionally relied on the provision of voluntary grant-in-aid funding to encourage state and local governments to perform particular activities or provide particular services that were deemed to be in the national interest. These arrangements were viewed as reflecting, at least in part, the constitutional protections afforded state and local governments as separate, sovereign entities. During the 1970s and 1980s, however, state and local government advocates argued that a "dramatic shift" occurred in the way the federal government dealt with states and localities. Instead of relying on the technique of subsidization to achieve its goals, the federal government was increasingly relying on "new, more intrusive, and more compulsory" programs and regulations that required compliance under the threat of civil or criminal penalties, imposed federal fiscal sanctions for failure to comply with the programs' requirements, or preempted state and local government authority to act in the area.[2] These new, more intrusive, and compulsory programs and regulations came to be referred to as "unfunded mandates" on states and localities.

State and local government advocates viewed these unfunded federal intergovernmental mandates as inconsistent with the traditional view of American federalism, which was based on cooperation, not compulsion. They argued that a federal statute was needed to forestall federal legislation and regulations that imposed obligations on state and local governments that resulted in higher costs and inefficiencies. UMRA's enactment in 1995 culminated years of effort by state and local government officials to control, if not eliminate, the imposition of unfunded federal mandates.

Advocates of regulatory reform adapted the concept of unfunded mandates to their view that federal regulations often impose financial burdens on private enterprise. Critics of government regulation of business argued that these regulations impose unfunded mandates on the private sector, just as federal programs and regulations impose fiscal obligations on state and local governments. As a result, various business organizations subject to increased federal regulation came to support state and local government efforts to enact federal legislation to control unfunded federal intergovernmental mandates. Private sector advocates argued that they, too, should be provided relief from what they viewed as burdensome federal regulations that hinder economic growth.[3] Subsequently, proposals to control unfunded mandates that were developed in the early 1990s contained provisions addressing not only federal intergovernmental mandates, but federal private sector mandates as well.

During floor debate on legislation that became UMRA, sponsors of the measure emphasized its role in bringing "our system of federalism back into balance, by serving as a check against the easy imposition of unfunded mandates."[4] Opponents argued that federal mandates may be necessary to achieve national objectives in areas where voluntary action by state and local governments or business failed to achieve desired results. See the **Appendix** for a more detailed examination of the rise of unfunded federal mandates as a national issue and of UMRA's legislative history.[5]

Summary of UMRA's Provisions

The congressional commitment to reshaping intergovernmental relations through UMRA is reflected in its eight statutory purposes:

(1) to strengthen the partnership between the Federal Government and State, local, and tribal governments;
(2) to end the imposition, in the absence of full consideration by Congress, of Federal mandates on State, local, and tribal governments without adequate Federal funding, in a manner that may displace other essential State, local, and tribal governmental priorities;
(3) to assist Congress in its consideration of proposed legislation establishing or revising Federal programs containing Federal mandates affecting State, local, and tribal governments, and the private sector by—(A) providing for the development of information about the nature and size of mandates in proposed legislation; and (B) establishing a mechanism to bring such information to the attention of the Senate and the House of Representatives before the Senate and the House of Representatives vote on proposed legislation;
(4) to promote informed and deliberate decisions by Congress on the appropriateness of Federal mandates in any particular instance;

(5) to require that Congress consider whether to provide funding to assist State, local, and tribal governments in complying with Federal mandates, to require analyses of the impact of private sector mandates, and through the dissemination of that information provide informed and deliberate decisions by Congress and Federal agencies and retain competitive balance between the public and private sectors;
(6) to establish a point-of-order vote on the consideration in the Senate and House of Representatives of legislation containing significant Federal intergovernmental mandates without providing adequate funding to comply with such mandates;
(7) to assist Federal agencies in their consideration of proposed regulations affecting State, local, and tribal governments, by—(A) requiring that Federal agencies develop a process to enable the elected and other officials of State, local, and tribal governments to provide input when Federal agencies are developing regulations; and (B) requiring that Federal agencies prepare and consider estimates of the budgetary impact of regulations containing Federal mandates upon State, local, and tribal governments and the private sector before adopting such regulations, and ensuring that small governments are given special consideration in that process; and
(8) to begin consideration of the effect of previously imposed Federal mandates, including the impact on State, local, and tribal governments of Federal court interpretations of Federal statutes and regulations that impose Federal intergovernmental mandates.[6]

To achieve its purposes, UMRA's Title I established a procedural framework to shape congressional deliberations concerning covered unfunded intergovernmental and private sector mandates. This framework requires CBO to estimate the direct mandate costs of intergovernmental mandates exceeding $50 million and of private sector mandates exceeding $100 million (in any fiscal year) proposed in any measure reported from committee. It also establishes a point of order against consideration of legislation that contained intergovernmental mandates with mandate costs estimated to exceed the threshold amount. In addition, Title II requires federal administrative agencies, unless otherwise prohibited by law, to assess the effects on state and local governments and the private sector of proposed and final federal rules and to prepare a written statement of estimated costs and benefits for any mandate requiring an expenditure exceeding $100 million in any given year. All threshold amounts under these provisions are adjusted annually for inflation.[7]

In general, the requirements of Titles I and II apply to any provision in legislation, statute, or regulation that would impose an enforceable duty upon state and local governments or the private sector. However, UMRA does not apply to conditions of federal assistance, duties stemming from participation in voluntary federal programs, rules issued by independent regulatory agencies, or rules issued without a general notice of proposed rulemaking. Exceptions also exist for rules and legislative provisions that cover individual constitutional rights, discrimination, emergency assistance, grant accounting and auditing procedures, national security, treaty obligations, and certain elements of Social Security legislation.[8]

UMRA's Title III also called for a review of federal intergovernmental mandates to be completed by the now-defunct U.S. Advisory Commission on Intergovernmental Relations (ACIR) within 18 months of enactment.[9] ACIR completed a preliminary report on federal intergovernmental mandates in January 1996, but the final report was not released.[10] Finally, UMRA's Title IV authorizes judicial review of federal agency compliance with Title II provisions.[11]

WHAT IS AN UNFUNDED FEDERAL MANDATE?

One of the first issues Congress faced when considering unfunded federal mandate legislation was how to define the concept. For example, during a November 3, 1993, congressional hearing on unfunded mandate legislation, Senator Judd Gregg argued,

> Any bill reported out this committee [Governmental Affairs] should precisely define what constitutes an unfunded federal mandate.... An appropriate definition is crucial because it will drive almost everything else that occurs. Without a precise definition, endless litigation would likely ensue over what is and what is not an unfunded federal mandate. A true solution to the problem cannot allow it to become more cost-effective to pay the bills than to seek payment. Furthermore, the definition cannot be too restrictive. It would solve nothing to cut off one particular type of unfunded mandate, only to prompt Congressional use of another to accelerate.[12]

The difficulty Congress faced in defining the concept was that there were strong disagreements, among academics, practitioners, and elected officials, over how to define it. These disagreements appear motivated by concerns about which classes of costs incurred by state and local governments (or the private sector) should be identified and controlled for in the legislative or regulatory process. They have typically been conducted, however, as disputes about which classes of such costs are properly considered as obligatory requirements on the affected entities. The resulting focus on whether or not particular kinds of costs are "mandatory" has tended to obscure consideration of the core policy question concerning what kinds of costs should be subjected to informational requirements or procedural restrictions such as those that UMRA establishes.

Competing Definitions

In 1979, one set of federalism scholars defined unfunded federal intergovernmental mandates broadly as including "any responsibility, action, procedure, or anything else that is imposed by constitutional, administrative, executive, or judicial action as a direct order or that is required as a condition of aid."[13] In 1984, ACIR offered a rationale for defining unfunded federal intergovernmental mandates which excluded conditions of aid. ACIR argued that defining unfunded federal intergovernmental mandates was difficult because federal grant-in-aid programs typically include both incentives and mandates backed by sanctions or penalties:

> Few federal programs affecting state and local governments are pure types.... Every grant-in-aid program, including General Revenue Sharing, the least restrictive form of aid, comes with federal "strings" attached. Here, as in other areas, there is no such thing as a free lunch.
>
> ... In the intergovernmental sphere, then, [mandates] and subsidy are less like different parts of a dichotomy than opposing ends of a continuum. At one extreme is the general support grant with just a few associated conditions or rules; at the other is the costly, but wholly unfunded, national "mandate." In between are many programs combining subsidy and [mandate] approaches, in varying degrees and in various ways.[14]

ACIR argued that because federal grant-in-aid programs typically combine subsidy and mandate approaches, grant-in-aid programs should be classified according to their degree of compulsion. It argued that conditions of grant aid should not be classified as a mandate because "one of the most important features of the grant-in-aid is that its acceptance is still viewed legally as entirely voluntary" and "although it is difficult for many jurisdictions to forego substantial financial benefits, this option remains real."[15] ACIR also argued that most grant conditions affect only the administration of those activities funded by the program, and "grants-in-aid generally provide significant benefits to the recipient jurisdiction."[16]

ACIR argued that federal grant-in-aid programs that "cannot be side-stepped, without incurring some federal sanction, by the simple expedient of refusing to participate in a single federal assistance program" should be considered mandates.[17] ACIR provided four examples of federal activities that, in the absence of sufficient compensatory funding, could be an unfunded intergovernmental mandate: (1) direct legal orders that must be complied with under the threat of civil or criminal penalties; (2) crosscutting or generally applicable requirements imposed on grants across the board to further national social and economic policies; (3) programs that impose federal fiscal sanctions in one program area or activity to influence state and local government policy in another area; and (4) federal preemption of state and local government law.[18]

In 1994, several organizations representing state and local governments issued a set of unfunded mandate principles which defined unfunded federal intergovernmental mandates as

- any federal requirement that compels state or local activities resulting in additional state or local expenditures;
- any federal requirement that imposes additional conditions or increases the level of state and local expenditures needed to maintain eligibility for existing federal grants;
- any reduction in the rate of federal matching for existing grants; and
- any federal requirement that reduces the productivity of existing state or local taxes and fees and/or that increases the cost of raising state and local revenue (including the costs of borrowing).[19]

Also in 1994, ACIR introduced the term "federally induced costs" to replace what it described as "the pejorative and definitional baggage associated with the term 'mandates.'"[20] ACIR identified the following types of federal activities that expose states and localities to additional costs:

- statutory direct orders;
- total and partial statutory preemptions;

- grant-in-aid conditions on spending and administration, including matching requirements;
- federal income tax provisions;
- federal court decisions; and
- administrative rules issued by federal agencies, including regulatory delays and non-enforcement.[21]

ACIR defended its inclusion of grant-in-aid conditions in its list of "federally induced costs," which it had excluded from its definition of federal mandates a decade earlier, by asserting that although the option of refusing to accept federal grants "seemed plausible when federal aid constituted a small and highly compartmentalized part of state and local revenues, it overlooks current realities. Many grant conditions have become far more integral to state and local activities—and far less subject to voluntary forbearance—than originally suggested by the contractual model."[22]

On April 28, 1994, John Kincaid, ACIR's executive director, testified at a congressional hearing that legislation concerning unfunded mandates "should recognize that unfunded Federal mandates include, in reality, a range of Federally-induced costs for which reimbursements may be legitimate considerations."[23] State and local government officials generally advocated the inclusion of ACIR's "federally induced costs" in legislation placing conditions on the imposition of unfunded intergovernmental mandates. However, organizations representing various environmental and social groups, such as the Committee on the Appointment of People With Disabilities, the Natural Resources Defense Council, the American Federation of State, County, and Municipal Employees, and the Service Employees International Union, argued that ACIR's definition was too broad. These groups testified at various congressional hearings that some federal mandates, particularly those involving the environment and constitutional rights, should be retained, even if they were unfunded.[24]

Statutory Direct Orders

With respect to definitions, there was, and continues to be, a general consensus among federalism scholars, state and local government officials, and other organizations that federal policies which impose unavoidable costs on state and local governments or business are, in the absence of sufficient compensatory funding, unfunded federal mandates. Because statutory direct orders, such as the Equal Employment Opportunity Act of 1972, which bars employment discrimination on the basis of race, color, religion, sex, and national origin, are compulsory, they are considered federal mandates. In the absence of sufficient compensatory funding, they are unfunded federal mandates. However, there was, and continues to be, a general consensus that some statutory direct orders, particularly those involving the guarantee of constitutional rights, should be exempt from legislation placing conditions on the imposition of unfunded federal mandates.[25] For example, on April 28, 1994, Governor (now Senator) Benjamin Nelson, testifying on behalf of the National Governors Association at a congressional hearing on unfunded mandate legislation, argued,

> At the outset, Mr. Chairman, I want to make it absolutely crystal clear that the Governors' position opposing unfunded environmental mandates must not be interpreted as an effort to discontinue environmental legislation and regulations or oppose any individual's civil or constitutional rights. The Governors consider the protection of public health and State natural resources as among the most important responsibilities of our office. We all take an oath of office to protect the health and safety of our citizens. In addition, we have worked with Congress over the years to enact strong Federal environmental laws.[26]

Total and Partial Statutory Preemptions

Total and partial preemptions of state and local spending and regulatory authority by the federal government are compulsory, but there was, and continues to be, disagreement concerning whether they should be considered federal mandates, or whether they should be included in legislation designed to provide relief from unfunded federal mandates. Total preemptions in the intergovernmental arena prevent state and local government officials from implementing their own programs in a policy area. For example, states have been "stripped of their powers to engage in economic regulation of airlines, bus, and trucking companies, to establish a compulsory retirement age for their employees other than specified state policymakers and judges, or to regulate bankruptcies with the exception of the establishment of a homestead exemption."[27]

Partial preemption typically is a joint enterprise, "whereby the federal government exerts its constitutional authority to preempt a field and establish minimum national standards, but allows regulatory administration to be delegated to the states if they adopt standards at least as strict as the federal rules."[28] Legally, the state decision to administer a partial preemption program is voluntary. States that do not have a program in a particular area or do not wish to assume the costs of administration and enforcement can opt out and allow the federal government to enforce the standards.[29] Nonetheless, the federal standards apply.

Total and partial statutory preemptions are distinct from unfunded federal intergovernmental mandates because they do not necessarily impose costs or require state and local governments to take action. Nonetheless, some federalism scholars and state and local government officials have argued that total and partial statutory preemptions should be included in legislation placing conditions on the imposition of unfunded federal mandates because they can have similar adverse effects on state and local government flexibilities and, in some instances, resources.[30] A leading federalism scholar identified 557 federal preemption statutes as of 2005.[31]

Others argue that because total and partial preemptions are distinct from unfunded federal mandates, they should not be included in legislation placing conditions on the imposition of unfunded federal mandates. In addition, some business organizations oppose including preemptions in any law or definition involving unfunded federal mandates because federal preemptions can result in the standardization of regulation across state and local jurisdictions, an outcome favored by some business interests, particularly those with interstate and global operations.[32]

Grant-in-Aid Conditions

Conditions of grants-in-aid are generally not considered unfunded mandates because the costs they impose on state and local governments can be avoided by refusing the grant. However, federalism scholars and state and local government officials have argued that, in the absence of sufficient compensatory funding, grant conditions should be considered unfunded federal intergovernmental mandates, even though the grants themselves are voluntary.[33] In their view, federal "grants often require major commitments of state resources, changes in state laws, and even constitutional provisions to conform to a host of federal policy and administrative requirements" and that some grant programs, such as Medicaid, are "too large for state and local governments to voluntarily turn down, or when new and onerous conditions are added some time after state and local governments have become dependent on the program."[34] For example, on April 28, 1994, Patrick Sweeney, a Democratic member of Ohio's state House of Representatives testifying on behalf of the National Conference of State Legislatures (NCSL), asserted at a congressional hearing on unfunded mandate legislation that

> A great majority of the current problem can be attributed to Federal entitlements that are defined but then not adequately funded, and the proliferation of a mandatory requirement for what previously were voluntary programs. Programs like Medicaid are voluntary in theory only. A State cannot unilaterally opt out of Medicaid at any time it wishes, once it is in the program, without having to obtain a Federal waiver or face certain lawsuits.[35]

Federal Tax Provisions

Federalism scholars, state and local government officials, and other organizations argue that federal tax policies that preempt state and local authority to tax specific activities or entities are unfunded mandates, and should be covered under legislation placing restrictions on unfunded mandates, because the fiscal impact of preempting state or local government revenue sources cannot be avoided and "can be every bit as costly" as mandates ordering state or local government action. [36] For example, the Internet Tax Freedom Act Amendments Act of 2007 extended the moratorium on internet taxation through November 1, 2014.[37] An academic study sponsored by the National Governors Association (NGA) and NCSL estimated that states could receive an additional $18 billion annually in state sales tax revenue if the moratorium were lifted.[38]

In addition, because most state and local income taxes have been designed purposively to conform with federal tax law, changes in federal tax policy can impact state and local government finances. For example, federal tax cuts adopted in 2001 and 2003 affecting depreciation, dividends, and estate taxes "forced states to acquiesce and accept their consequences or decouple from the federal tax base."[39] Yet, federal tax changes are generally considered not to be unfunded mandates because states and localities can avoid their costs by decoupling their income tax from the federal income tax. Nevertheless, because federal tax changes can affect state and local government tax bases, most state and local government officials advocate their inclusion in federal legislation placing conditions on the imposition of unfunded federal mandates.

Federal Court Decisions; Administrative Rules Issued by Federal Agencies; and Regulatory Delays and Non-enforcement

Federalism scholars, state and local government officials, and other organizations argue that, in the absence of sufficient compensatory funding, court decisions and regulatory actions taken by federal agencies, including regulatory delays and non-enforcement, are unfunded mandates and should be included in legislation placing conditions on the imposition of unfunded mandates because these actions can impose costs on state and local governments that cannot be avoided. UMRA's provisions concerning administrative rules are discussed in greater detail later in this chapter (see the section on "UMRA and Federal Rulemaking (Title II)").

UMRA's Definition of an Unfunded Federal Mandate

After taking various definitions into consideration, Congress defined federal mandates in UMRA more narrowly than state and local government officials had hoped. Federal intergovernmental mandates were defined as any provision in legislation, statute, or regulation that "would impose an enforceable duty upon State, local, or tribal governments" or "reduce or eliminate the amount" of federal funding authorized to cover the costs of an existing mandate.[40] Provisions in legislation, statute, or regulation that "would increase the stringency of conditions of assistance" or "would place caps upon, or otherwise decrease" federal funding for existing intergovernmental grants with annual entitlement authority of $500 million or more could also be considered a federal intergovernmental mandate, but only if the state, local, or tribal government "lack authority under that program to amend their financial or programmatic responsibilities to continue providing required services that are affected by the legislation, statute, or regulation."[41]

Private sector mandates were defined as "any provision in legislation, statute, or regulation that would impose an enforceable duty upon the private sector" or "reduce or eliminate the amount" of federal funding authorized "for the purposes of ensuring compliance with such duty." [42]

Key words in both definitions are "enforceable duty." Because statutory direct orders, total and partial preemptions, federal tax policies that preempt specific state and local tax policies, and administrative rules issued by federal agencies cannot be avoided, they are enforceable duties and are covered under UMRA. In contrast, because federal grants are voluntary, grant conditions are not considered enforceable duties and, therefore, are not covered under UMRA. Federal tax policies that impose costs on state and local governments that can be avoided by decoupling the state or local government's affected income tax provision from the federal income tax code are not enforceable duties, and, therefore, also are not covered under UMRA.

UMRA considers a mandate unfunded unless the legislation authorizing the mandate fully meets its estimated direct costs by either (1) providing new budget authority (direct spending authority or entitlement authority) or (2) authorizing appropriations. If appropriations are authorized, the mandate is still considered unfunded unless the legislation ensures that in any fiscal year, either: (1) the actual costs of the mandate are estimated not to exceed the appropriations actually provided; (2) the terms of the mandate will be revised so that it can be carried out with the funds appropriated; (3) the mandate will be abolished; or (4) Congress will enact new legislation to continue the mandate as an unfunded mandate.[43] This mechanism for reviewing and revising mandates on the basis of their actual costs, which was introduced into UMRA in the "Byrd look- back amendment" (as described in the **Appendix**), applies only to intergovernmental mandates enacted in legislation as funded through appropriations.

Exemptions and Exclusions

UMRA generally excluded pre-existing federal mandates from its provisions, but, as mentioned previously, it did include any provision in legislation, statute, or regulation that "would increase the stringency of conditions of assistance" or "would place caps upon, or otherwise decrease" federal funding for existing intergovernmental grants with annual entitlement authority of $500 million or more.[44] However, this provision applies "only if the state or locality lacks authority to amend its financial or programmatic responsibilities to continue providing the required services."[45] Because CBO has determined that many large intergovernmental entitlement grant programs, such as Medicaid and Temporary Assistance to Needy Families, "allow states significant flexibility to alter their programs and accommodate new requirements," UMRA provisions have not been applied to them.[46]

UMRA's Title I does not apply to conditions of federal assistance; duties stemming from participation in voluntary federal programs; and legislative provisions that cover individual constitutional rights, discrimination, emergency assistance, grant accounting and auditing procedures, national security, treaty obligations, and certain parts of Social Security relating to the old-age, survivors, and disability insurance program under title II of the Social Security Act.[47]

UMRA did not indicate that these exempted provisions and rules were not federal mandates. Instead, it established that their costs would not be subject to its provisions requiring written cost estimate statements, or to its provisions permitting a point of order to be raised against the consideration of reported legislation in which they appear. The Senate Committee on Governmental Affairs report accompanying S. 1, The Unfunded Mandate Reform Act of 1995, provided its reasoning for adopting the exempted provisions and rules:

Table 1. Congressional Budget Office Estimates of Costs of Intergovernmental Mandates, 104th - 111 th Congresses

Congress	Cost Estimate Statements Transmitted	Statements With Identified Intergovernmental Mandates	Intergovernmental Mandate Costs Exceeding the Threshold	CBO Unable to Determine Mandate Costs
104th (1996)	718	69	11	6
105th (1997-1998)	1,062	128	14	14
106th (1999-2000)	1,279	158	7	1
107th (2001-2002)	1,038	110	10	8
108th (2003-2004)	1,172	152	16	7
109th (2005-2006)	978	171	18	6
110th (2007-2008)	1,382	168	7	6
111th (2009-2010)	1,074	124	11	17
Total	**8,703**	**1,080**	**94**	**65**

Sources: U.S. Congressional Budget Office, "Cost Estimates," December 6, 2010, http://www.cbo.gov/search/ ce_sitesearch.cfm; U.S. Congressional Budget Office, *A Review of CBO's Activities in 2008 Under the Unfunded Mandates Reform Act*, March 2009, p. 21; and U.S. Congressional Budget Office, *A Review of CBO's Activities Under the Unfunded Mandates Reform Act, 1996 to 2005*, March 2006, p. 4.

Notes: CBO began preparing mandate statements in January 1996. The figures for the 104th Congress reflect bills on the legislative calendar in January 1996 and bills reported by authorizing committees thereafter.

A number of these exemptions are standard in many pieces of legislation in order to recognize the domain of the President in foreign affairs and as Commander-in-Chief as well as to ensure that Congress's and the Executive Branch's hands are not tied with procedural requirements in times of national emergencies. Further, the Committee thinks that Federal auditing, accounting and other similar requirements designed to protect Federal funds from potential waste, fraud, and abuse should be exempt from the Act.

The Committee recognizes the special circumstances and history surrounding the enactment and enforcement of Federal civil rights laws. During the middle part of the 20th century, the arguments of those who opposed the national, uniform extension of basic equal rights, protection, and

> opportunity to all individuals were based on a States rights philosophy. With the passage of the Civil Rights Acts of 1957 and 1964 and the Voting Rights Act of 1965, Congress rejected that argument out of hand as designed to thwart equal opportunity and to protect discriminatory, unjust and unfair practices in the treatment of individuals in certain parts of the country. The Committee therefore exempts Federal civil rights laws from the requirements of this Act.[48]

In addition, as will be discussed in the next section, UMRA does not require all legislative provisions that contain federal mandates, even those that contain mandates that meet UMRA's definition, to have a CBO written cost estimate statement. In some instances, CBO may determine that cost estimates may not be feasible or complete. In addition, UMRA only requires estimates of direct costs imposed by the legislation. Estimates of indirect, secondary costs, such as effects on prices and wages when the costs of a mandate imposed on one party are passed on to others, such as customers or employees, are not required.[49]

UMRA and Congressional Procedure (Title I)

UMRA's Procedures

Under Title I, which took effect on January 1, 1996, CBO was directed, to the extent practicable, to assist congressional committees, upon their request, in analyzing the budgetary and financial impact of any proposed legislation that may have (1) a significant budgetary impact on state, local, and tribal governments; (2) a significant financial impact on the private sector; or (3) a significant employment impact on the private sector. In addition, CBO was directed, if asked by a committee chair or committee ranking minority member, to conduct a study, to the extent practicable, of the budgetary and financial impact of proposed legislation containing a federal mandate. If reasonably feasible, the study is to include estimates of the future direct costs of the federal mandate "to the extent that such costs significantly differ from or extend beyond the 5- year period after the mandate is first effective."[50]

While the actions noted above are technically discretionary, UMRA does contain mandatory directives. When an authorizing committee reports a public bill or joint resolution containing a federal mandate, UMRA requires the committee to provide the measure to CBO for budgetary analysis.[51] CBO is required to provide the committee a cost estimate statement of a mandate's direct costs if those costs are estimated to equal or exceed predetermined amounts, adjusted for inflation, in any of the first five fiscal years the legislation would be in effect. In 2010, those threshold amounts are $70 million for intergovernmental mandates and $141 million for private sector mandates. CBO is also required to inform the committee if the mandate has estimated direct costs below these thresholds and briefly explain the basis of the estimate.

CBO must also identify any increase in federal appropriations or other spending that has been provided to fund the mandate.[52] The federal mandate is considered unfunded unless estimated costs are fully funded. As described above, under "UMRA's Definition of an Unfunded Federal Mandate," UMRA provides that mandate costs be considered as funded only if the legislation covers the mandate costs either by providing new direct spending or entitlement authority or by authorizing appropriations and incorporating a mechanism to provide for the mandate to be revised or abolished if the requisite appropriations are not provided.

Direct costs for intergovernmental mandates are defined as "the aggregate estimated amounts that all State, local and tribal governments would be required to spend or would be prohibited from raising in revenues in order to comply with the Federal intergovernmental mandate."[53] Direct costs for federal private sector mandates are defined as "the aggregate estimated amounts that the private sector will be required to spend in order to comply with the Federal private sector mandate."[54]

To accomplish these tasks, CBO created the State and Local Government Cost Estimates Unit within its Budget Analysis Division to prepare intergovernmental mandate cost estimate statements as well as other analysis and special studies on the budgetary effects of mandates. It also added new staff to its program analysis divisions to prepare private sector mandate cost estimate statements.[55]

A congressional committee is required to include the CBO estimate of mandate costs in its report on the bill. If the mandate cost estimate is not available, or if the report is not expected to be in print before the legislation reaches the floor for consideration, the committee is to publish the mandate cost estimate in the *Congressional Record* in advance of floor consideration. In addition to identifying direct costs, the committee's report must also assess the likely costs and benefits of any mandates in the legislation, describe how they affect the competitive balance between the private and public sectors, state the extent to which the legislation would preempt state, local or tribal law, and explain the effect of any preemption. For intergovernmental mandates alone, the committee is to describe in its report the extent to which the legislation authorizes federal funding for direct costs of the mandate, and detail whether and how funding is to be provided. [56]

CBO Cost Estimate Statements

As indicated in **Table 1**, CBO has submitted 8,703 estimates of mandate costs to Congress from January 1, 1996, when UMRA's Title I became effective, to December 6, 2010. Each of these statements examined the mandate costs imposed on the private sector and/or state, local, and tribal governments by provisions in a specific bill, amendment, or conference report. About 12.4% of these cost estimate statements (1,080 of 8,703 cost estimate statements) identified costs imposed by intergovernmental mandates on states and localities, and 1.1% of them (94 of 8,703 cost estimate statements) identified intergovernmental mandates that exceeded UMRA's threshold. CBO was unable to determine costs imposed by intergovernmental mandates in 61 bills, amendments, or conference reports.

As indicated in **Table 2**, CBO has submitted 8,581 estimates to Congress that examined private sector mandate costs imposed by provisions in a specific bill, amendment, or conference report from January 1, 1996, when UMRA's Title I became effective, to December 6, 2010. The number of statements transmitted to Congress shown in **Table 2** is less than the number shown in **Table 1** because CBO is sometimes asked to review a specific bill, amendment, or conference report solely for intergovernmental mandates.

About 14.9% of these private sector estimates (1,281 of 8,581 cost estimate statements) identified costs imposed by mandates, and 3.7% of them (314 of 8,581 cost estimate statements) identified costs that exceeded UMRA's threshold. CBO was unable to determine costs imposed by private sector mandates in 190 bills, amendments, or conference reports.

Points of Order for Initial Consideration

UMRA provides for the enforcement of its informational requirements on legislation by establishing a point of order in each chamber against consideration of a measure on which the reporting committee has not published the required estimate of mandate costs. This point of order applies only to measures reported by committees (for which CBO estimates of mandate costs are required), but it applies for both intergovernmental and private sector mandates. In addition, however, if the informational requirement is met, a point of order against consideration of a measure may still be raised, if, for any fiscal year, the estimated total mandate cost of unfunded intergovernmental mandates in the measure exceeds UMRA's threshold amount ($70 million in 2010). This point of order may be raised also if CBO reported that no reasonable estimate of the cost of intergovernmental mandates was feasible.[57]

Table 2. Congressional Budget Office Estimate of Costs of Private Sector Mandates, 104th - 111th Congresses

Congress	Cost Estimate Statements Transmitted	Statements With Identified Private Sector Mandates	Private Sector Mandate Costs Exceeding the Threshold	CBO Unable to Determine Mandate Costs
104th (1996)	673	91	38	2
105th (1997-1998)	1,023	140	36	14
106th (1999-2000)	1,253	191	26	20
107th (2001-2002)	1,034	139	37	22
108th (2003-2004)	1,168	171	38	28
109th (2005-2006)	974	184	45	32
110th (2007-2008)	1,382	256	67	47
111th (2009-2010)	1,074	109	27	31
Total	8,581	1,281	314	196

Source: U.S. Congressional Budget Office, "Cost Estimates," December 6, 2010, http://www.cbo.gov/search/ ce_sitesearch.cfm; U.S. Congressional Budget Office, *A Review of CBO's Activities in 2008 Under the Unfunded Mandates Reform Act*, March 2009, p. 21; and U.S. Congressional Budget Office, *A Review of CBO's Activities Under the Unfunded Mandates Reform Act, 1996 to 2005*, March 2006, p. 4.

Notes: CBO began preparing mandate statements in January 1996. The figures for the 104th Congress reflect bills on the legislative calendar in January 1996 and bills reported by authorizing committees thereafter. In some years, CBO transmitted more cost estimate statements for intergovernmental mandates than private sector mandates because sometimes CBO was asked to review a specific bill, amendment, or conference report solely for intergovernmental mandates.

Uniquely among the requirements established by UMRA, this substantive point of order addressing intergovernmental mandates contained in legislation constitutes a potential means of control over the actual imposition of mandate costs. Even in this case, however, the mechanisms established by UMRA provide a means of controlling mandates only on the basis of estimates of the costs that will be incurred in subsequent fiscal years. The only provision of UMRA that offers a possibility of controls based on costs actually incurred by affected entities is the requirement, mentioned earlier, that a mandate can be considered funded through appropriations only if it directs that, if insufficient appropriations are made, the mandate must be revised, abolished, or reenacted as unfunded.

In several respects, the applicability of the substantive point of order differs from that of the informational point of order. First, it applies to any measure coming to the floor for consideration, whether or not reported by a committee, and also to conference reports. For a measure that has been reported, this point of order applies to the measure in the form reported, including, for example, to a committee amendment in the nature of a substitute. In addition, this point of order applies against an amendment or motion (such as a motion to recommit with amendatory instructions), and does so on the basis not that the mandate costs of the amendment or motion itself exceeds the threshold, but that the amendment or motion would cause the total mandate costs in the measure to do so. Finally, however, this point of order applies only against intergovernmental mandates. UMRA imposes no comparable control in relation to private sector mandates.

Because federal mandates are created through authorization bills, the UMRA points of order generally do not apply to bills reported by the House and Senate Committees on Appropriations. However, if an appropriation bill, resolution, amendment, or conference report contains legislative provisions that would either increase the direct costs of a federal intergovernmental mandate that exceeds the threshold, or cause those costs to exceed the threshold, a point of order may be raised against the provisions themselves. In the Senate, if this point of order is sustained, the provisions are stricken from the bill.[58]

In the House, the chair does not rule on a point of order raised under these provisions. Instead, the House, by majority vote, determines whether to consider the measure despite the point of order. To prevent dilatory use of the point of order, the chair need not put the question of consideration to a vote unless the member making the point of order meets the "threshold burden" of identifying specific language that is claimed to contain the unfunded mandate.

Also, if several points of order could be raised against the same measure, House practices under UMRA allow all of them to be disposed of at once by a single vote on consideration. If the Committee on Rules proposes a special rule for considering the measure that waives the point of order, UMRA subjects the special rule itself to a point of order, which is disposed of by the same mechanism.[59]

In the Senate, if questions are raised challenging the applicability of an UMRA point of order (e.g., to prevent its use for dilatory purposes), the presiding officer, to the extent practicable, consults with the Committee on Homeland Security and Governmental Affairs to determine if the measure contains an intergovernmental mandate and with the Senate Committee on the Budget to determine if the mandate's direct costs meet UMRA's threshold for allowing a point of order to be raised. The Senate Committee on the Budget may draw for this purpose on CBO cost estimate statements. If there are no such challenges, or the presiding officer rules against the challenge, the Senate determines whether to consider the measure despite the point of order. It may do so by voting on a motion to waive the point of order.[60]

Initially, a majority vote was necessary to waive the point of order in the Senate.[61] In 2005, the Senate increased its threshold to waive an UMRA point of order to 60 votes. Two UMRA points of order were raised in the Senate that year, and both were sustained, defeating two amendments to an appropriations bill that would have increased the minimum wage (see **Table 3**). In 2007, the Senate lowered its threshold to waive an UMRA point of order to a majority vote.[62]

A scholar familiar with UMRA has argued that, inasmuch as the general floor procedures of the Senate already allowed Senators to force a majority vote on a mandate by moving to strike it from the bill, UMRA's enforcement procedure of waiving a point of order by majority vote meant that UMRA mattered only in the House.[63] As evidence of this, the scholar noted that during UMRA's first 10 years of operation, when the threshold to waive an UMRA point of order was a majority vote in both the House and Senate, 13 UMRA points of order were raised, all in the House (see **Table 3**).

As indicated in **Table 3**, 39 UMRA points of order have been raised in the House. Only one of these points of order, the first one, which was raised on March 28, 1996, in opposition to a proposal to add a minimum wage increase to the Contract With America Advancement Act of 1996, resulted in the House voting to reject consideration of a proposed provision. During the 111th Congress, UMRA points of order in the House have generally been raised not to challenge unfunded federal mandates *per se*, but to use the 10 minutes of debate allowed each House member initiating an UMRA point of order to challenge the pace of legislative consideration, limitations on the offering of amendments to appropriations bills, or the inclusion of earmarks in legislation.[64]

Table 3. UMRA Points of Order in the House and Senate, by Congress

Congress	Points of Order Raised in the House	Points of Order Sustained in the House	Points of Order Raised in the Senate	Points of Order Sustained in the Senate	Congress
104th	(1996)	3	1	0	0
105th	(1997-1998)	4	0	0	0
106th	(1999-2000)	4	0	0	0
107th	(2001-2002)	2	0	0	0
108th (2003-2004)	0	0	0		0
109th (2005-2006)	6	0	2		2
110th (2007-2008)	8	0	0		0
111th (2009-)	12	0	1		0
Total	39	1	3	2	

Source: Rep. Bill Archer, "Contract With America Advancement Act of 1996," House debate on motion to recommit H.R. 3136, *Congressional Record*, vol. 142, part 5 (March 28, 1996), pp. 6931-6937; Rep. Rob Portman, "The Employee Commuting Act of 1996," House debate on H.R. 1227, *Congressional Record*, vol. 142, part 9 (May 23, 1996), pp. 12283-12287; Rep. Bill Orton, "The Welfare – Medicaid Reform Act of 1996," House debate on H.R. 3734, *Congressional Record*, vol. 142, part 13 (July 18, 1996), p. 17668; Rep. Melvin Watt, "The Housing Opportunity and Responsibility Act," House debate on H.R. 2, *Congressional Record*, vol. 143, part 5 (May 1, 1997), pp. 7006-7012; Rep. John Ensign, "The Nuclear Waste Policy Act of 1997," House debate on H.R, 1270, *Congressional Record*, vol. 143, no, 148 (October 29, 1997), pp. H9655-H9657; Rep. Gerald Soloman, "The Agricultural Research, Extension, and Education Reform Act of 1998," House debate on the conference report for S. 1150, *Congressional Record*, vol. 144, part 8 (June 4, 1998), pp. H9655-H9657; Rep. Jerrold Nadler, "The Bankruptcy Reform Act of 1998," House debate on H.R. 3150, *Congressional Record*, vol. 144, part 8 (June 10, 1998), pp. 11853-11857; Rep. Steve Largent, "The Minimum Wage Increase Act," House debate on H.R. 3846, *Congressional Record*, vol. 144, part 2 (March 9, 2000), pp. 2623-2624;

Rep. James Gibbons, "The Nuclear Waste Policy Amendments Act of 2000," House debate on S. 1287, *Congressional Record*, vol. 146, part 2 (March 22, 2000), pp. 3234-3236; Rep. John Conyers, "The Internet Nondiscrimination Act of 2000," House debate on H.R. 3709, *Congressional Record*, vol. 146, part 6 (May 10, 2000), pp. 7483-7485; Rep. Charles Stenholm, "The Medicare RX 2000 Act," House debate on H.R. 4680, *Congressional Record*, vol. 146, part 9 (June 28, 2000), pp. 12650-12653; Rep. Jim Moran, "The Department of Transportation Appropriations Act, 2002," House debate on H.R. 2299, *Congressional Record*, vol. 147, part 9 (June 26, 2001), pp. 11906-11910; Rep. James Gibbons, "The Yucca Mountain Repository Site Approval Act," House debate on H.J.Res. 87, *Congressional Record*, vol. 148, part 5 (May 8, 2002), pp. 7145-7148; Rep. Sheila Jackson-Lee, "The Real ID Act of 2005," House debate on H.R. 418, *Congressional Record*, vol. 151, no. 13 (February 9, 2005), pp. H437-H442; Rep. James McGovern, "The Energy Policy Act of 2005," House debate on H.R. 6, *Congressional Record*, vol. 151, no. 48 (April 20, 2005), pp. H2 174-H2 178; Sen. Kit Bond, "The Transportation, Treasury, HUD and Independent Agencies Appropriations Act, 2006," Senate debate on H.R. 3058, *Congressional Record*, vol. 151, no. 133 (October 19, 2005), p. S1 1547; Sen. Ted Kennedy, "The Transportation, Treasury, HUD and Independent Agencies Appropriations Act, 2006," Senate debate on H.R. 3058, *Congressional Record*, vol. 151, no. 133 (October 19, 2005), p. S1 1548; Rep. Jim McDermott, "The Deficit Reduction Act of 2005," House debate on H.R. 4241, *Congressional Record*, vol. 151, no. 152 (November 17, 2005), pp. H 10531-H1 0534; Rep. Jim McDermott, "The Deficit Reduction Act of 2005," House debate on H.Res. 653, *Congressional Record*, vol. 152, no. 10 (February 1, 2006), pp. H37-H40; Rep. Tammy Baldwin, "The Communications Opportunity, Promotion, and Enhancement Act of 2006," House debate on H.R. 5252, *Congressional Record*, vol. 152, no. 72 (June 8, 2006), pp. H3506-H35 10; Rep. Jim McDermott, "The Federal Election Integrity Act of 2006," House debate on H.R. 4844, *Congressional Record*, vol. 152, no. 118 (September 20, 2006), pp. H6742-H6745; Rep. Pete Sessions, "The Children's Health and Medicare Protections Act of 2007," House debate on H.R. 3162, *Congressional Record*, vol. 153, no. 124-125 (August 1, 2007), pp. H9288-H9290; Rep. Pete Sessions, "The Children's Health Insurance Program Reauthorization Act of 2007," House debate on H.R. 3963, *Congressional Record*, vol. 153, no. 163 (October 25, 2007), pp. H 12027-H1 2029; Rep. Jeff Flake, "Senate Amendments to H.R. 6, Energy Independence and Security Act of 2007," House debate on H.R. 6, *Congressional Record*, vol. 153, no. 186 (December 6, 2007), pp. H4255-H4259; Rep. Mike Conaway, "The Renewable Energy and Energy Conservation Tax Act of 2008," House debate on H.R. 5351, *Congressional Record*, vol. 154, no. 32 (February 27, 2008), pp. H 1079-H 1082; Rep. Paul Broun, "The Paul Wellstone Mental Health and Addiction Equity Act of 2007," House debate on H.R. 1424, *Congressional Record*, vol. 154, no. 37 (March 5, 2008), pp. H 1259-H 1262; Rep. Jeff Flake, "The Food, Conservation, and Energy Act of 2008," House debate on H.R. 2419, *Congressional Record*, vol. 154, no. 79 (May 14, 2008), pp. H3784-H3789; Rep. Eric Cantor, "The Comprehensive American Energy Security and Consumer Protection Act," House debate on H.R. 6899, *Congressional Record*, vol. 154, no. 147 (September 16, 2008), pp. H8 1 52-H 8157; Rep. Jeff Flake, "The Consolidated Security, Disaster Assistance and Continuing Appropriations Act, 2009," House debate on H.R. 2638, *Congressional Record*, vol. 154, no. 152 (September 24, 2008), pp. H92 1 8-H9220; Rep. David Drier, "The American Recovery and Reinvestment Act," House debate on H.R. 1, *Congressional Record*, vol. 155, no. 30 (February 13, 2009), pp. H 1524-H 1536; Rep. Jeff Flake, "The Omnibus Appropriations Act, 2009," House debate on H.R. 1105, *Congressional Record*, vol. 155, no. 33 (February 25, 2009), pp. H2643-H2646; Rep. Jeff Flake, "The Agriculture, Rural Development, Food and Drug Administration Appropriations Act, 2009," House debate on H.R. 2997, *Congressional Record*, vol. 155, no. 101 (July 8, 2009), pp. H7783-H7786; Rep. Jeff Flake, "The Military Construction and Veteran's Affairs Appropriations Act, 2010," House debate on H.R. 3082, *Congressional Record*, vol. 155, no. 103 (July 10, 2009), pp. H795 1 -H7953; Rep. Jeff Flake, "The Energy and Water Development Appropriations Act, 2010," House debate on H.R. 3183, *Congressional Record*, vol. 155, no. 106 (July 15, 2009), pp. H8 1 07-H8 109; Rep. Jeff Flake, "The Financial Services and General Government Appropriations Act, 2010," House debate on H.R. 3170, *Congressional Record*, vol. 155, no. 107 (July 16, 2009), pp. H8191-H8193; Rep. Jeff Flake, "The Transportation, Housing and Urban Development Appropriations Act, 2010," House debate on H.R. 3288, *Congressional Record*, vol. 155, no. 112 (July 23, 2009), pp. H8593-H8594; Rep. Jeff Flake, "The Departments of Labor, Health, and Human Services, and Education Appropriations Act, 2010," House debate on H.R. 3293, *Congressional Record*, vol. 155, no. 113 (July 24, 2009), pp. H8593-H8594; Rep. Jeff Flake, "The Department of Defense Appropriations Act, 2010," House debate on H.R. 3326, *Congressional Record*, vol. 155, no. 116 (July 29, 2009), pp. H8977-H8978; Senator Robert Corker, "H.R. 3590, the Service Members Home Ownership Act of 2009," remarks in the Senate, *Congressional Record*, daily edition, vol. 155, no. 199 (December 23, 2009), pp. S 13803- S 13804; Rep. Paul Ryan, "Providing for Consideration of Senate Amendments to H.R. 3590, Service Members Home Ownership Tax Act of 2009, and Providing for Consideration of H.R. 4872, Health Care and Education Reconciliation Act of 2010," House debate on H.Res. 1203, *Congressional Record*, daily edition, vol. 156, no. 43 (March 21, 2010), pp. H 1825-H1 828; Rep. Jeff Flake, "Providing For Consideration of H.R. 5822, Military Construction and Veterans Affairs and Related Agencies Appropriations Act, 2011," House debate on H.R. 5822, *Congressional Record*, vol. 156, no. 112 (July 28, 2010), pp. H6206-H6209; and Rep. Jeff Flake, "Providing For Consideration of H.R. 5850, Transportation, Housing And Urban Development, and Related Agencies Appropriations Act,

2011," House debate on H.R. 5850, *Congressional Record*, vol. 156, no. 113 (July 29, 2010), pp. H6298-H6290.

Also, as indicated in **Table 3**, UMRA points of order have been raised in the Senate three times. In 2005, points of order were raised against two amendments relating to an increase in the minimum wage. In each case the Senate declined to waive the point of order, and the chair ruled that the amendment was out of order because it contained unfunded intergovernmental mandates in excess of the threshold.[65] In 2009, an UMRA point of order was raised against intergovernmental mandates in a health care reform bill.[66] The Senate voted to waive the point of order, 55-44.[67] The Senate subsequently approved the bill with the mandates.[68]

Impact on the Enactment of Statutory Intergovernmental and Private Sector Mandates

Although UMRA points of order have been sustained just three times, most state and local government officials assert that UMRA has reduced "the number of unfunded federal mandates by acting as a deterrent to their enactment."[69] For example, NCSL's policy position on unfunded federal mandates asserts that

> Title I of UMRA—requiring the Congress to perform cost estimates and providing for a point of order—has been successful in reducing the number of unfunded mandates passed by the Congress. Further, the unfunded mandate point of order and other procedural mechanisms contained in UMRA have proven to be effective without impeding the legislative process.[70]

Also, Raymond Scheppach, NGA's executive director, testified before a House subcommittee in 2001 that UMRA has slowed the growth of unfunded mandates and improved communications between federal policymakers and state and local government officials:

> Direct mandates have declined sharply in the wake of the Act. But I would venture that UMRA has had an even greater intangible benefit. As Congressman Portman once told us, he was certain this would be one of those bills that he could frame and hang on his wall, and it would become just another relic of history. But, to his surprise, the Act has led – time and again—to members asking his advice: "Do you think this bill will cause an

> UMRA problem? With whom should I work?" The very threat of a CBO report has engendered efforts to reach out to state and local leaders before the fact—instead of after. It has changed the nature of our intergovernmental discussion in a very positive way.[71]

In addition, there have been documented instances in which either sponsors of legislation have modified provisions to avoid a CBO statement that unfunded intergovernmental mandate costs exceeded the threshold, or measures with such costs estimated to exceed the threshold were altered prior to floor consideration to reduce their costs below the threshold.[72]

As mentioned previously, since UMRA's Title I became effective in 1996, CBO has submitted 8,703 written cost estimate statements to Congress that examined the costs imposed by provisions in a specific bill, amendment, or conference report on the private sector and/or state and local governments. It identified intergovernmental mandates in 1,080 of them (12.4%). CBO also reported in March 2010 that "only 11" of the 91 bills that it identified from 1996 through 2009 as having intergovernmental mandate costs above UMRA's threshold were enacted.[73] Those mandates are as follows:

- Two increases in the minimum wage—P.L. 104-188, enacted in 1996, was estimated to cost state and local governments more than $1 billion during the first five years that it was in effect. P.L. 110-28, enacted in 2007, was estimated to cost state and local governments slightly less than $1 billion during the first five years that it was in effect.
- A reduction in federal funding for administering the food stamp program, now the Supplemental Nutrition Assistance Program, P.L. 105-185, enacted in 1998, was estimated to cost states between $200 million and $300 million annually.
- Preemption of state taxes on premiums for certain prescription drug plans, P.L. 108-73, enacted in 2003, was estimated to cost states $70 million in revenue in 2006, the first year it was in effect, and increase to about $95 million annually by 2010.
- The temporary preemption of states' authority to tax certain Internet services and transactions, P.L. 108-435, enacted in 2004, was estimated to reduce state and local government tax revenue by at least $300 million; the extension of this preemption in P.L. 110-108, enacted in 2007, was estimated to reduce state and local government tax revenue by about $80 million annually.

- The requirement that state and local governments meet certain standards for issuing driver's licenses, identification cards, and vital statistics documents, P.L. 108-458, enacted in 2004, was estimated to cost state and local governments more than $100 million over 2005-2009, with costs exceeding the threshold in at least one of those years.
- The elimination of matching federal payments for some child support spending, P.L. 109-171, enacted in 2006, was estimated to cost states more than $100 million annually beginning in 2008.
- The requirement that state and local governments withhold taxes on certain payments for property and services, P.L. 109-222, enacted in 2006, was estimated to cost state and local governments more than $70 million annually beginning in 2011.
- Requirements on rail and transit owners and operators to train workers and submit reports to the Department of Homeland Security, P.L. 110-53, enacted in 2007, was estimated to cost state and local governments more than UMRA's threshold in at least one of the first five years following enactment.
- The requirement that commuter railroads install train-control technology, P.L. 110-432, enacted in 2008, was estimated to cost state and local governments more than UMRA's threshold in at least one of the first five years following enactment.[74]

State and local government interest groups argue that these statistics confirm UMRA's effectiveness in serving as a deterrent to the enactment of new unfunded mandates that exceed UMRA's threshold and meet UMRA's definition of a federal mandate. However, they also argue that many mandates with costs below UMRA's threshold, or that do not meet UMRA's definition of a federal mandate, have been adopted since UMRA's enactment.[75] CBO reports that from 2004 through 2009, 167 new intergovernmental federal mandates and 248 new private sector mandates with identified costs below UMRA's threshold were enacted; and hundreds of other bills were identified as having an effect on state and local government budgets, but those bills did not meet UMRA's definition of a federal mandate.[76]

As mentioned previously, CBO reported that it has submitted 8,581 cost estimate statements to Congress that examined the costs imposed by provisions in a specific bill, amendment, or conference report that might impact the private sector. It identified private sector mandates in 1,281 of them (14.9%). It also reported in March 2010 that 84 of the 314 bills that it identified from 1996 through 2009 as having private sector mandate costs above UMRA's threshold were enacted. Of these 84 measures, 46 involved either taxes or fees.[77]

Congressional Issues for Title I

Exemptions and Exclusions

State and local government officials argue that UMRA's exemptions and exclusions reduce its effectiveness in limiting the enactment of unfunded federal intergovernmental mandates. They argue that federal programs in the exempted and excluded areas can still result in the imposition of costs on state, local, and tribal governments. Also, because UMRA does not include these costs as "mandates," they are exempt even from the requirement for CBO to estimate these costs. For example, in 2008, NCSL asserted that "although fewer than a dozen mandates have been enacted that exceed the threshold established in UMRA, Congress has shifted at least $131 billion in costs to states over the past five years" and that during the 110th Congress at least $31 billion in additional costs were imposed on states through new mandates.[78]

To reduce these costs, NCSL has recommended that UMRA's provisions on points of order and requirements for written cost estimate statements also apply to (1) all open-ended entitlement grant-in-aid programs, such as Medicaid, and legislative provisions that would cap or enforce a ceiling on the cost of federal participation in any entitlement or mandatory spending program; (2) new conditions of federal funding for existing federal grants and programs; (3) legislative provisions that reduce state revenues, especially when changes to the federal tax code are retroactive or otherwise provide states with little or no opportunity to prospectively address the impact of a change in federal law on state revenues; and (4) mandates that fail to exceed the statutory threshold only because they do not affect all states.[79]

For the most part, business interests have generally supported state and local government officials in their efforts to broaden UMRA's coverage of federal intergovernmental mandates. In perhaps the most extensive effort to obtain various viewpoints on UMRA, in 2005, the Government Accountability Office (GAO) held group meetings, individual interviews, and received written responses from 52 individuals and organizations, including academic centers and think tanks, businesses, federal agencies, public interest advocacy groups, and state and local governments, concerning unfunded mandates. GAO reported that UMRA's coverage was the issue most frequently commented on by parties from all five sectors, including business, and that most of the parties representing business viewed UMRA's relatively narrow coverage as a major weakness that leaves out many federal actions with potentially significant financial impacts on nonfederal parties.[80] However, GAO also found that the business sector has "generally been in favor of federal preemptions for reasons such as standardizing regulation across state and local jurisdictions."[81]

Although GAO found that most of the parties it contacted viewed UMRA's coverage of intergovernmental mandates as being too narrow, it also reported that some of the participants opposed an expansion of UMRA's coverage:

> A few parties from the public interest sector and academic/think tank sectors considered some of the existing exclusions important or identified UMRA's narrow scope as one of the act's strengths.... Specifically, these parties argued in favor of maintaining UMRA's exclusions or expanding them to include federal actions regarding public health, safety, environmental protection, workers' rights, and the disabled.... [They also] focused on the importance of the existing exclusions, particularly those dealing with constitutional and statutory rights, such as those barring discrimination against various groups.[82]

With respect to private sector mandates in legislation, UMRA currently allows a point of order to be raised only if UMRA's informational requirements are not met; that is, only if the committee reporting the measure fails to publish a CBO cost estimate statement of the private sector mandate's costs. Over the years, various business organizations, including the U.S. Chamber of Commerce, have advocated the extension of UMRA's substantive point of order for intergovernmental mandates to the private sector, permitting a point of order to be raised against consideration of legislation that includes private sector mandates with costs that exceed UMRA's threshold.[83]

The GAO report also noted that "parties primarily from the academic/ think tank and state and local governments sectors ... noted that while much attention has been focused on the actual (direct) costs of mandates, it is important to consider the broader implications on affected nonfederal entities beyond direct costs, including indirect costs such as opportunity costs, forgone revenues, shifting priorities, and fiscal trade-offs."[84]

UMRA AND FEDERAL RULEMAKING (TITLE II)

UMRA's Title II, which became effective on March 22, 1995, generally requires federal agencies, unless otherwise prohibited by law, to prepare written statements that identify costs and benefits of a federal mandate to be imposed through the rulemaking process that may result in the expenditure by state, local, and tribal governments, in the aggregate, or by the private sector, of $100 million or more (adjusted annually for inflation) in any one year, before "promulgating any general notice of proposed rulemaking."[85] In 2010, the threshold for preparing a written statement is $141 million. These informational requirements for regulations, like the Title I cost estimate requirements for legislation, apply to both intergovernmental and private sector mandates. Title II establishes no equivalent to the point of order mechanism in Title I through which either house can decline to consider legislation proposing covered unfunded intergovernmental mandates above the applicable threshold level.

The written assessments that federal agencies are to prepare for their regulations must identify the law authorizing the rule and include a qualitative and quantitative assessment of anticipated costs and benefits, the share of costs to be borne by the federal government, and the disproportionate budgetary effects upon particular regions, state, local, or tribal governments, or particular segments of the private sector. Assessments must also include estimates of the effect on the national economy, descriptions of consultations with nonfederal government officials, and a summary of the evaluation of comments and concerns obtained throughout the promulgation process.[86] Impacts of "any regulatory requirements" on small governments must be identified, notice must be given to those governments, and technical assistance must be provided.[87] Also, federal agencies are required, to the extent permitted in law, to develop an "effective process to permit elected officers of State, local, and tribal governments (or their designated employees with authority to act on their behalf) to provide meaningful and timely input in the development of regulatory proposals containing significant Federal intergovernmental mandates."[88] UMRA also requires federal agencies to consider "a reasonable number" of regulatory alternatives and select the "least costly, most cost-effective or least burdensome alternative" that achieves the objectives of the rule.[89]

UMRA requires the Office of Management and Budget's (OMB) director to collect the executive branch agencies' written cost estimate statements and periodically forward copies to CBO's director. It also directs OMB to establish pilot programs in at least two federal agencies to test innovative regulatory approaches to reduce regulatory burdens on small governments, and provide Congress a written annual report detailing compliance with the act by each agency for the preceding reporting period.[90] OMB's director has delegated these responsibilities to its Office of Information and Regulatory Affairs (OIRA).

Most of these provisions were already in place when UMRA was adopted. For example, Executive Order 12866, issued in September 1993, required agencies to provide OIRA with assessments of the costs and benefits of all economically significant proposed rules (defined as having an annual impact on the economy of $100 million or more), including some rules that were not mandates; to identify regulatory alternatives and explain why the planned regulatory action is preferable to other alternatives; to issue regulations that were cost-effective and impose the least burden on society; and to seek the views of state, local, and tribal officials before imposing regulatory requirements that might significantly or uniquely affect them.[91]

Title II's Exemptions and Exclusions

UMRA's requirement for federal agencies to issue written cost estimate statements for mandates issued through the rulemaking process that may result in expenditures of $100 million or more (adjusted annually for inflation) by state and local governments, in the aggregate, or by the private sector, in any one year, is subject to the exemptions and exclusions that apply to legislative provisions (e.g., conditions of federal assistance, duties arising from participation in a voluntary federal program, constitutional rights of individuals etc.). In addition, UMRA's requirements do not apply (1) to provisions in rules issued by independent regulatory agencies; (2) if the agency is "otherwise prohibited by law" from considering estimates of costs in adopting the rule (e.g., under the Clean Air Act the primary air quality standards are health-based and the courts have affirmed that the U.S. Environmental Protection Agency is not to consider costs in determining air quality standards for ozone and particulate matter); or (3) to any rule for which the agency does not publish a general notice of proposed rulemaking in the *Federal Register*.[92] GAO has found that about half of all final rules published in the *Federal Register* are published without a general notice of proposed rulemaking, including some rules with impacts over $100 million annually.[93]

In addition, UMRA's threshold for federal mandates in rules is limited to expenditures, in contrast to the thresholds in Title I which refer to direct costs. As a result, a federal rule's estimated annual effect on direct costs might meet Title I's threshold, but might not meet Title II's threshold if the rule does not compel nonfederal entities to spend that amount. For example, under Title I, direct costs include any amounts that state and local governments are prohibited from raising in revenue to comply with the mandate. These costs are not considered when determining whether a mandate meets Title II's threshold because funds not received are not expenditures.[94]

Also, in contrast to Title I, Title II does not require the agencies issuing regulations to address the question of whether federal funding is available to cover the costs to the private sector of mandates imposed by regulations. In general, agencies lack authority to provide such funding, which could be provided only by legislative action. Title II addresses the funding only of intergovernmental mandates, and only by requiring that agencies identify the extent to which federal resources may be available to carry out those mandates.[95] The differences in the coverage of Title I and Title II may reflect a compromise reached with congressional members who opposed using UMRA as a vehicle to address broader regulatory reform advocated by business interests. For example, Senator John Glenn argued in the Senate Committee on Governmental Affairs' committee report on UMRA:

> Another problematic change from S. 993 is the expansion of the "regulatory accountability and reform" provisions of Title 2 to go beyond intergovernmental mandates to address any and all regulatory effects on the private sector. The intended purpose of S. 1 is to control unfunded Federal mandates on State and local governments. I have always supported that goal. Moreover, I believe that if we keep the bill sharply focused on that purpose, we can get the legislation passed quickly and signed into law. If, however, we let the bill be stretched to cover other issues, we hurt prospects for enactment and we break our pledge to our friends in the State and local governments.... I believe that the bill should be brought back to its original purpose by limiting regulatory analysis to intergovernmental mandates.... In short, I support using this legislation to control intergovernmental regulatory costs. I oppose using this bill to address broader regulatory reform issues.[96]

Federal Agency Cost Estimate Statements in Major Federal Rules

From March 22, 1995, when UMRA's Title II became effective, to the end of FY2009, OMB reviewed 642 final rules with estimated benefits and/or costs exceeding $100 million annually.[97] Most (72%) of those "major" rules (463) did not contain provisions meeting UMRA's definition of a mandate. Whereas, as **Table 1** and **Table 2** show, CBO identified slightly more private sector mandates than intergovernmental mandates, **Table 4** shows that most of the mandates identified in regulations have been directed at the private sector. This emphasis appears consistent with the original concern of business advocates to extend the concept of mandates to the area of regulatory reform. As indicated in **Table 4**, during the time period covered, 170 major rules met UMRA's definition of a mandate on the private sector and, therefore, were issued an UMRA cost estimate statement and 9 met UMRA's definition of a mandate on state, local, and tribal governments and, therefore, were issued an UMRA cost estimate statement.

Table 4. UMRA Written Mandate Cost Estimate Statements Issued by Federal Agencies in Final Rules, 1995-2009

Time Period	Private Sector Mandates	Public Sector Mandates	Total
June 1995 -May 2000	76	4	80
June 2000 -May 2001	16	2	18
May 2001- October 2001	4	0	4
October 2001 - September 2002	5	0	5
October 2002 - September 2003	17	0	17
October 2003 - September 2004	10	0	10
October 2004 - September 2005	3	1	4
October 2005 - September 2006	9	1	10
October 2006 - September 2007	11	0	11
October 2007 - September 2008	8	0	8
October 2008 - September 2009	11	1	12
Total	170	9	179

Sources: Joint Hearing, U.S. Congress, House Committee on Government Reform, Subcommittee on Energy Policy, Natural Resources and Regulatory Affairs, and House Committee on Rules, Subcommittee on Technology and the House, *Unfunded Mandates: A Five Year Review and Recommendations for Change*, hearing on the Unfunded Mandates Reform Act of 1995, 107th Cong., 1st sess., May 24, 2001, H. Hrg. 107-19 (Washington: GPO, 2001), p. 40; U.S. Office of Management and Budget, *Making Sense of Regulation: 2001 Report to Congress on the Costs and Benefits of Regulations and Unfunded Mandates on State, Local, and Tribal Entities*, Washington, DC, December 2001, pp. 189-195; U.S. Office of Management and Budget, *Stimulating Smarter Regulation: 2002 Report to Congress on the Costs and Benefits of Regulations and Unfunded Mandates on State, Local, and Tribal Entities*, Washington, DC, December 2002, pp. 161, 162; U.S. Office of Management and Budget, *Informing Regulatory Decisions: 2003 Report to Congress on the Costs and Benefits of Regulations and Unfunded Mandates on State, Local, and Tribal Entities*, Washington, DC, September 2003, pp. 202-204; U.S. Office of Management and Budget, *Progress in Regulatory Reform: 2004 Report to Congress on the Costs and Benefits of Regulations and Unfunded Mandates on State, Local, and Tribal Entities*, Washington, DC, December 2004, pp. 225-234; U.S. Office of Management and Budget, *Validating Regulatory Analysis: 2005 Report to Congress on the Costs and Benefits of Regulations and Unfunded Mandates on State, Local, and Tribal Entities*, Washington, DC, December 2005, pp. 143-148; U.S. Office of Management and Budget, *2006 Report to Congress on the Costs and Benefits of Regulations and Unfunded Mandates on State, Local, and Tribal Entities*, Washington, DC, January 2007, pp. 14 1-143; U.S. Office of Management and Budget, *2007 Report to Congress on the Costs and Benefits of Regulations and Unfunded Mandates on State, Local, and Tribal Entities*, Washington, DC, June 2008, pp. 76-81; U.S. Office of Management and Budget, *2008 Report to Congress on the Costs and Benefits of Regulations and Unfunded Mandates on State, Local, and Tribal Entities*, Washington, DC, January 2009, pp. 77-81; U.S. Office of Management and Budget, *2009 Report to Congress on the Benefits and Costs of Federal Regulations and Unfunded Mandates on State, Local, and Tribal Entities*, Washington, DC, January 27, 2010, pp. 62-65; and U.S. Office of Management and Budget, *2010 Report to Congress on the Benefits and Costs of Federal Regulations and Unfunded Mandates on State, Local, and Tribal Entities*, Washington, DC, July 20, 2010, pp. 73-79.

The nine intergovernmental rules, eight issued by the U.S. Environmental Protection Agency (EPA), were as follows:

- EPA's Rule on Standards of Performance for Municipal Waste Combustors and Emissions Guidelines (1995), with estimated costs of $320 million annually;
- EPA's Standards of Performance for New Stationary Sources and Guidelines for Control of Existing Sources: Municipal Solid Waste Landfills (1996), with estimated costs of $110 million annually;

- EPA's National Primary Drinking Water Regulations: Disinfectants and Disinfection Byproducts (1998), with estimated costs of $700 million annually;
- EPA's National Primary Drinking Water Regulations: Interim Enhanced Surface Water Treatment (1998), with estimated costs of $300 million annually;
- EPA's National Pollutant Discharge Elimination: System B Regulations for Revision of the Water Pollution Control Program Addressing Storm Water Discharges (1999), with estimated costs of $803.1 million annually;
- EPA's National Primary Drinking Water Regulations; Arsenic and Clarifications to Compliance and New Source Contaminants Monitoring (2001), with estimated costs of $206 million annually;
- EPA's National Primary Drinking Water Regulations: Long Term 2 Enhanced Surface Water Treatment (2005), with estimated costs between $60 million and $170 million per year;
- EPA's National Primary Drinking Water Regulations: Stage 2 Disinfection Byproducts Rule (2006), with estimated costs of at least $100 million annually, and
- Health Insurance Reform; Modifications to the Health Insurance Portability and Accountability Act (HIPAA) Electronic Transaction Standards (2009), with estimated costs of $1.1 billion.[98]

Impact on the Rulemaking Process

In 1997, Senators Fred Thompson and John Glenn, chair and ranking minority member of the Senate Committee on Governmental Affairs, respectively, asked GAO to review federal agencies' implementation of UMRA's Title II. On February 4, 1998, GAO issued its report, concluding that "our review of federal agencies' implementation of Title II of UMRA indicates that this title of the act has had little direct effect on agencies' rulemaking actions during the first 2 years of its implementation."[99]

GAO concluded that Title II had limited impact on agencies' rulemaking primarily because of its limited coverage. For example, GAO noted that written mandate cost estimate statements were not on file at CBO for 80 of the 110 economically significant rules published in the *Federal Register* between March 22, 1995 and March 22, 1997. GAO examined the 80 economically significant rules that lacked a written mandate cost estimate statement and concluded that UMRA did not require a written mandate cost estimate statement for 78 of them because the rule either did not have an associated notice of proposed rulemaking (18 instances); did not impose an enforceable duty (3 instances); imposed such a duty but only as a condition of federal assistance (33 instances); imposed such a duty but only as part of a voluntary program (11 instances); did not involve an expenditure of $100 million in any single year by the private sector or by state, local, and tribal governments (12 instances); or incorporated requirements specifically set forth in law (one instance). GAO concluded that written mandate cost estimate statements should have been filed at CBO for two of the rules that lacked one, but, in both instances, the rules appeared to satisfy UMRA's written statement requirements.[100]

Even where UMRA applied, GAO concluded that the act did not appear to have had much effect on federal agencies' rulemaking actions because UMRA does not require agencies to take the actions required in the statute if the agencies determine that the actions are duplicative of other actions or that accurate estimates of the rule's future compliance costs are not feasible.[101] Because federal agencies' rules commonly contain an estimate of compliance costs, GAO found that most agencies rarely prepared a separate UMRA written cost estimate statement. Moreover, Executive Order 12866, which was issued more than a year before UMRA's enactment, already required federal agencies to provide OIRA with assessments of the costs and benefits of all economically significant rules. GAO also concluded that UMRA did not substantially change agencies' intergovernmental consultation processes.[102]

In 2001, OMB's director, Mitchell L. Daniels, Jr., acknowledged at a House hearing coinciding with UMRA's fifth anniversary that UMRA's Title II had not resulted in major changes in federal agency rulemaking. He noted that, according to OMB's five annual reports to Congress on the implementation of Title II, 80 rules had required the preparation of a separate written mandate cost estimate statement (see **Table 4**). He said that "it was hard to believe that only 80 regulations had significant impacts on state, local, or tribal governments, or the private sector. In fact, it appears that agencies have attempted to limit their consultative processes, and ignored potential alternative remedies, by aggressively utilizing the exemptions outlined by the Act."[103] He added that "when agencies fail to solicit or consider the views of states and localities, they deny themselves the benefit of state and local innovation and experience. This will not be accepted practice in this [George W. Bush] Administration."[104]

In 2004, GAO released a second study of UMRA's implementation of Title II (and the first for Title I), focusing on statutes enacted and rules published during 2001 and 2002. GAO found that 5 of 377 statutes enacted and 9 of 122 major or economically significant final rules issued in 2001 or 2002 were identified as containing federal mandates at or above UMRA's thresholds.[105] GAO concluded its report by stating that "the findings raise the question of whether UMRA's procedures, definitions, and exclusions adequately capture and subject to scrutiny federal statutory and regulatory actions that might impose significant financial burdens on affected nonfederal parties."[106]

As noted earlier, in 2005, GAO sought and received input from participating parties about UMRA's strengths and weaknesses and potential options for reinforcing the strengths or addressing the weaknesses. It also held a symposium on federal mandates to examine those identified strengths and weaknesses in more depth. [107] Although the symposium's participants viewed UMRA's coverage as its most significant issue, GAO reported that comments received concerning federal agency consultation with state and local governments under Title II "focused on the quality of consultations across agencies, which was viewed as inconsistent" and that "a few parties commented that UMRA had improved consultation and collaboration between federal agencies and nonfederal levels of government."[108]

At a Senate hearing held on April 14, 2005, OIRA's director, John Graham, testified that OMB includes summaries of agency consultations with state and local government officials in its annual report to Congress and that "this year's report shows an increased level of engagement."[109] He added that there were "some very good examples of consultation that are documented in that report at the Department of Education, the Environmental Protection Agency and so forth, but I think that it would be fair to say that those best practices are not necessarily uniform across the federal government or across any particular agency."[110] State and local government officials testifying at the hearing stated that federal agency consultation had improved somewhat, but remained "sporadic."[111]

Congressional Issues for Title II

Exemptions and Exclusions

State and local government public interest groups continue to advocate a broadening of Title II's coverage. For example, as mentioned previously, they advocate a broader definition of what UMRA considers a mandate, under the presumption that a broader definition would subject more rules to Title II. An alternative approach would be to separate debates concerning the definition of "mandate" and UMRA's coverage, and, instead, apply Title II's information requirements to whatever classes of federally induced costs Congress deems appropriate to cover. This approach might be implemented by incorporating coverage of various kinds of "federally induced costs," adopting the terminology proposed earlier by ACIR, as mentioned previously. In either case, inasmuch as Title II's requirements are informational only, their extension to new classes of regulations, or to new kinds of federally induced costs, would not affect the authority of agencies to issue regulations or the substance of the regulations that could be issued.

State and local government advocacy groups have also argued that Title II should apply to rules issued by independent regulatory agencies.[112] Although OMB does not review rules issued by independent regulatory agencies, in recent years it has included information concerning independent regulatory agency rules in its annual UMRA report to Congress. According to those reports, independent regulatory agencies issued 139 major rules from FY1997 through FY2008.[113]

In addition, the National Association of Counties (NACO) and other state and local government public interest groups have advocated a strengthening of OMB's role in the enforcement of Title II to ensure consistent application of UMRA's provisions across federal agencies.[114] For example, NCSL's current policy statement on unfunded mandates asserts that Title II "has been only marginally effective in reducing costly and administratively cumbersome rules and regulations on states and localities" and recommends that it be amended to include "the creation of an office within the Office of Management and Budget that is analogous to the State and Local Government Cost Estimates Unit at the Congressional Budget Office." [115] Business organizations, led by the U.S. Chamber of Commerce, also have advocated an independent review of federal agency cost estimates, recommending that the reviews be conducted by OMB or GAO. They also have advocated the permitting of early judicial challenges to an agency's failure to complete an UMRA cost estimate statement or for completing one that is deficient.[116]

As mentioned previously, organizations representing various environmental and social groups have argued that UMRA has achieved its stated goals of strengthening the partnership between the federal government and state, local, and tribal governments by promoting informed and deliberate decisions by Congress on the appropriateness of federal mandates. In their view, broadening UMRA's coverage would dilute its impact. For example, a participant at GAO's 2005 symposium on federal mandates argued that eliminating any of UMRA's exclusions and exemptions might make the identification of mandates less meaningful, saying "The more red flags run up, the less important the red flag becomes."[117] Also, some of the participants at the symposium from the academic, policy research institute, and public interest advocacy sectors argued that it was essential that some of the existing exclusions, such as those dealing with constitutional and statutory rights barring discrimination against various groups, be retained. They also advocated additional exclusions to include federal actions regarding public health, safety, environmental protection, workers' rights, and the disabled.[118]

Federal Agency Consultation Requirements

State and local government public interest groups assert that enhanced requirements for federal agency consultation with state and local government officials during the rulemaking process are needed.[119] For example, NCSL's current policy statement asserts that federal agency "consultation with state and local governments in the construction of these rules is haphazard" and recommends that Title II be amended to include "enhanced requirements for federal agencies to consult with state and local governments."[120]

OMB asserts that "federal agencies have been actively consulting with states, localities, and tribal governments in order to ensure that regulatory activities were conducted consistent with the requirements of the Act."[121] In addition, OMB notes that it has had guidelines in place since September 21, 1995, to assist federal agencies in complying with the act.[122] The current guidelines suggest that (1) intergovernmental consultations should take place as early as possible, beginning before issuance of a proposed rule and continuing through the final rule stage, and be integrated explicitly into the rulemaking process; (2) agencies should consult with a wide variety of state, local, and tribal officials; (3) agencies should estimate direct benefits and costs to assist with these consultations; (4) the scope of consultation should reflect the cost and significance of the mandate being considered; (5) effective consultation requires trust and significant and sustained attention so that all who participate can enjoy frank discussion and focus on key priorities; and (6) agencies should seek out state, local, and tribal views on costs, benefits, risks, and alternative methods of compliance, and whether the federal rule will harmonize with and not duplicate similar laws in other levels of government.[123]

OMB has also argued that it includes summaries of selected consultation activities by agencies whose actions affect state, local and tribal governments in its annual UMRA report to Congress and those summaries indicate that federal agencies are complying with the act. For example, in its 2008 UMRA report to Congress, OMB wrote in the introduction to these summaries:

> Five agencies (the Departments of Energy, Education, Commerce, Housing and Urban Development, and the Environmental Protection Agency) have provided examples of consultation activities that involved State, local and tribal governments not only in their regulatory processes, but also in their program planning and implementation phases. These agencies have worked to enhance the regulatory environment by improving the way in which the Federal Government relates to its intergovernmental partners. In general, many of the departments and agencies not listed here (including the Departments of Justice, State, Treasury, and Veterans Affairs, the Small Business Administration, and the General Services Administration) do not often impose mandates upon States, localities or tribes, and thus have fewer occasions to consult with these governments.
>
> ... Federal agencies conduct a wide range of consultations. Agency consultations sometimes involve multiple levels of government, depending on the agency's understanding of the scope and impact of the rule. OMB continues to work with agencies to ensure that consultation occurs with the appropriate level of government.[124]

CONCLUDING OBSERVATIONS

In 1995, UMRA's enactment was considered an historic, milestone event in the history of American intergovernmental relations. For example, when signing UMRA, President Bill Clinton said,

> Today, we are making history. We are working to find the right balance for the 21st century. We are recognizing that the pendulum had swung too far, and that we have to rely on the initiative, the creativity, the determination, and the decisionmaking of people at the State and local level to carry much of the load for America as we move into the 21st century.[125]

Since UMRA's enactment, parties participating in its implementation and researchers in the academic community, policy research institutes, and nonpartisan government agencies have reached different conclusions concerning the extent of UMRA's impact on intergovernmental relations and whether UMRA should be amended. State and local government officials and federalism scholars generally view UMRA as having a limited, though positive, impact on intergovernmental relations. In their view, the federal government has continued to expand its authority through the "carrots" of increased federal assistance and the "sticks" of grant conditions, preemptions, mandates, and administrative rulemaking. Facing what they view as a seemingly ever growing federal influence in American governance, they generally advocate a broadening of UMRA's coverage to enhance its impact, emphasizing the need to include conditions of grant assistance and a broader range of federal agency rulemaking, including rules issued by independent regulatory agencies. Reflecting these views, on May 5, 2009, Representative Virginia Foxx introduced legislation, H.R. 2255, that would, among other things, broaden UMRA's coverage to include an assessment of the costs of conditions of federal financial assistance and reasonably foreseeable indirect costs .[126] Also, on July 22, 2010, Representative Scott Garrett introduced legislation, H.R. 5818, to make private sector mandates subject to a point of order.[127]

Other organizations, representing various environmental and social groups, argue that UMRA's coverage does not need to be broadened. In their view, UMRA has accomplished its goals of fostering improved intergovernmental relations and ensuring that when Congress votes on major federal mandates it is aware of the costs imposed by the legislation. They assert that UMRA's current limits on coverage should be maintained or reinforced by adding exclusions for mandates regarding public health, safety, workers' rights, environmental protection, and the disabled. [128]

During the 111th Congress, UMRA received increased attention as Congress considered various proposals to reform health care. Governors, for example, expressed opposition to proposals that would have required states to contribute toward the cost of expanding Medicaid eligibility, asserting that the expansion could inflate state deficits and impose on states what Tennessee Governor Philip Bredesen reportedly described as the "mother of all unfunded mandates."[129] However, as mentioned previously, proposals to expand Medicaid eligibility are not covered by UMRA because it has been determined that states "have significant flexibility to make programmatic adjustments in their Medicaid programs to accommodate" new federal requirements.[130]

Underlying disagreements over UMRA's future are fundamentally different values concerning American federalism. One view emphasizes the importance of freeing state and local government officials from the constraints brought about by the directives and costs associated with federal mandates so they can experiment with innovative ways to achieve results with greater efficiency and cost effectiveness. This view focuses on the positive effect active state and local governments can have in promoting a sense of state and community responsibility and self-reliance, encouraging participation and civic responsibility by allowing more people to become involved in public questions, adapting public programs to state and local needs and conditions, and reducing the political turmoil that sometimes results from single policies that govern the entire nation.[131]

Another view emphasizes the federal government's responsibility to ensure that all citizens are afforded minimum levels of essential government services. This view focuses on the propensity of states to restrict governmental services because they compete with one another for businesses and taxpaying residents; the variation in state fiscal capacities that make it difficult for some states to provide certain governmental services even though they might have the political will to do so; and the propensity of states to have different views concerning what services are essential and what constitutes a sufficient level of essential government services.[132]

Given these disagreements over fundamental values, it is perhaps not surprising that there are differences of opinion concerning UMRA's future. Using President Clinton's words, debates over UMRA's future are more than just arguments over who will pay for what; they are also about finding "the right balance" for American federalism in the 21st century.

APPENDIX. THE RISE OF UNFUNDED MANDATES AS A NATIONAL ISSUE AND UMRA'S LEGISLATIVE HISTORY

Unfunded mandates became a national issue during the 1980s as state and local government officials and their affiliated public interest groups, led by the National League of Cities (NLC), U.S. Conference of Mayors (USCM), and National Association of Counties (NACO), began an intensive lobbying effort to limit unfunded intergovernmental mandates. Their efforts were supported by various business organizations, led by the U.S. Chamber of Commerce, which opposed the imposition of unfunded mandates on both state and local governments and the private sector, particularly mandates issued through federal rules.[133]

Increased Number and Cost of Unfunded Mandates

State and local government officials became involved in the issue of unfunded federal mandates during the 1980s primarily because the number and costs of unfunded intergovernmental mandates were increasing and, by then, nearly every community in the nation had become subject to their effects. For example, ACIR reported that during the 1980s the costs of unfunded intergovernmental mandates were increasing at a rate faster than federal assistance. ACIR also identified 63 federal statutes as of 1990 that, in its view, imposed "major" restrictions or costs on state and local governments. Many of the statutes involved civil rights, consumer protection, improved health and safety, and environmental protection.[134] Only two of the 63 statutes it identified, the Davis-Bacon Act of 1931 and Hatch Act of 1940, were enacted prior to 1964, 9 were enacted during the 1960s, 25 during the 1970s, 21 during the 1980s, and 6 in 1990. A study completed by the Clinton Administration's National Performance Review identified 172 laws in force that imposed requirements (regardless of the magnitude of their impact) on state and local governments as of December 1992.[135]

Some of the major federal statutes adopted during the 1970s that imposed relatively costly federal mandates on state and local governments were the Equal Employment Opportunity Act of 1972, which extended the prohibitions against discrimination in employment contained in the Civil Rights Act of 1964 to state and local government employment; the Fair Labor Standards Act Amendments of 1974, which extended the prohibitions against age discrimination in the Age Discrimination in Employment Act of 1967 to state and local government employment; and the Public Utilities Regulatory Policy Act of 1978, which established federal requirements concerning the pricing of electricity and natural gas.[136] One of the more costly federal mandates enacted during the 1970s was Section 504 of the Rehabilitation Act of 1973. It prohibited discrimination against handicapped persons in federally assisted programs. CBO estimated that it would require states and localities to spend $6.8 billion over 30 years to equip buses with wheelchair lifts, to install elevators in subway systems, and to expand access to public transit systems for the physically disabled.[137]

Three of the more costly unfunded federal mandates adopted during the 1980s were the Safe Drinking Water Act Amendments of 1986 (which was estimated to impose an additional cost of between $2 billion and $3 billion on state and local governments to improve public water systems); the Asbestos Hazard Emergency Response Act of 1986 (which required schools to remove hazardous asbestos at an estimated cost of $3.15 billion over 30 years); and the Water Quality Act of 1987 (which was estimated to cost states and localities about $12 billion in capital costs for wastewater treatment).[138] ACIR estimated that new federal mandates adopted between 1983 and 1990 cost state and local governments between $8.9 billion and $12.7 billion, depending on the definition of mandate used; in FY1991, federal mandates imposed estimated costs of between $2.2 billion and $3.6 billion on state and local governments; and additional mandates, not included in these estimates, were scheduled to take effect in the years ahead.[139]

ACIR suggested that the expansion of federal intergovernmental mandates during the 1960s, 1970s, and 1980s fundamentally changed the nature of intergovernmental relations in the United States:

> During the 1960s and 1970s, state and local governments for the first time were brought under extensive federal regulatory controls.... Over this period, national controls have been adopted affecting public functions and services ranging from automobile inspection, animal preservation and college athletics to waste treatment and waste disposal. In field after field the power to set standards and determine methods of compliance has shifted from the states and localities to Washington.[140]

State and Local Governments Seek Relief from Unfunded Mandates

Edward I. Koch, then mayor of New York City and a former member of Congress, was one of the first public officials to highlight the mandate issue. In 1980, he authored an article criticizing what he called "the mandate millstone."[141] He noted that as a member of Congress he voted for many federal mandates "with every confidence that we were enacting sensible permanent solutions to critical problems" but now that he was a mayor he had come to realize that "over the past decade, a maze of complex statutory and administrative directives has come to threaten both the initiative and the financial health of local governments throughout the country."[142]

The continued growth in the number and cost of federal mandates during the 1980s and early 1990s generated renewed and heightened opposition from state and local government officials and their affiliated public interest groups. This opposition culminated in the National Unfunded Mandates (NUM) Day initiative, sponsored by the NLC, USCM, NACO, and International City/

County Management Association. Held on October 27, 1993, local government officials across the nation held press conferences and public forums criticizing unfunded mandates, and released a study of the costs imposed by federal mandates on local governments. Over 300 cities and 128 counties participated in the study, which, when extrapolated nationally, estimated that federal mandates imposed additional costs of $6.5 billion annually for cities and $4.8 billion annually for counties.[143]

The NUM Day methodology used to estimate the costs of unfunded federal mandates was later challenged because of the absence of independent validation of local government submissions and the non-random nature of the participating jurisdictions. However, politically, NUM Day was considered a success by its organizers for two reasons. First, it attracted unprecedented media attention to the issue of unfunded federal mandates. For example, the number of newspaper articles discussing unfunded federal mandates increased from 22 in 1992, to 179 in 1993, and to 836 in 1994.[144] Second, it increased congressional awareness of state and local government concerns about unfunded mandates. For example, on January 5, 1995, Senator John Glenn mentioned NUM Day as having an impact on congressional awareness of unfunded mandates at a Senate congressional hearing on S. 1—The Unfunded Mandate Reform Act:

> On October 27, 1993, State and local elected officials from all over the Nation came to Washington and declared that day—"National Unfunded Mandates Day." These officials conveyed a powerful message to Congress and the Clinton Administration on the need for Federal mandate reform and relief. They raised four major objections to unfunded Federal mandates.
>
> First, unfunded Federal mandates impose unreasonable fiscal burdens on their budgets;
>
> Second, they limit State and local government flexibility to address more pressing local problems like crime and education;
>
> Third, Federal mandates too often come in a "one-size-fits-all" box that stifles the development of more innovative local efforts—efforts that ultimately may be more effective in solving the problem the Federal Mandate is meant to address; and Fourth, they allow Congress to get credit for passing some worthy mandate or program, while leaving State and local governments with the difficult tasks of cutting services or raising taxes in order to pay for it.[145]

State and local government officials continued to lobby Congress for mandate relief legislation and coordinated their efforts to increase public awareness of their concerns. For example, on March 21, 1994, state and local government officials across the nation held town hall meetings and their affiliated public interest groups sponsored a rally on the Capitol steps to draw media attention to their concerns about unfunded federal mandates. The NLC and state municipal leagues across the country also declared October 24-30, 1994, Unfunded Mandates Week, which also generated considerable media coverage. [146]

The Initial Congressional Response

The efforts of state and local government officials appeared to have an effect on congressional legislative activity concerning unfunded federal mandates. During the 102nd Congress (1991- 1992), 12 federal mandate relief bills were introduced in the House and 10 were introduced in the Senate. All of these bills failed to be reported out of committee, and only one had a congressional hearing. During the first session of the 103rd Congress (1993), 32 federal mandate relief bills were introduced and one of them, S. 993, the Federal Mandate Accountability and Reform Act of 1994 co-sponsored by Senators John Glenn and Dirk Kempthorne, was reported by the Senate Governmental Affairs Committee on June 16, 1994. It contained several provisions that were later in UMRA, and included an amendment offered by Senator Byron Dorgan "to include the private sector under the CBO and Committee mandate cost analysis requirements of Title I of S. 993, and a Glenn amendment to allow CBO to waive the private sector cost analysis if CBO cannot make a "reasonable estimate" of the bills cost."[147] The bill was considered by the Senate on October 6, 1994, without a time agreement. After the introduction of several amendments and some debate, the Senate proceeded to other issues and adjourned without voting on the measure. [148] The House Government Operations Committee also reported a bill, H.R. 5128, the Federal Mandates Relief for State and Local Government Act of 1994, sponsored by Representative John Conyers, Jr., on October 5, 1994. It was similar to S. 993, but its approval was delayed, reportedly due to concerns raised by several senior Democratic members worried that mandate legislation might make it more difficult to adopt laws to protect the environment and address social issues. Congress adjourned before the bill could move to the floor for consideration. [149]

Core Federalism Principles Debated During UMRA's Consideration

The Republican Party gained control of the House of Representatives for the first time in 40 years following the congressional elections held on November 8, 1994. They also achieved a slim majority in the Senate as well. [150] Mandate reform was a key provision in the Republican Party's "Contract With America."[151] Perhaps reflecting its importance to the Republican leadership, the prospective Senate majority leader, Senator Robert Dole, designated a revised unfunded mandate relief bill, co-sponsored by Senators Kempthorne and Glenn and introduced on January 4, 1995, the opening day of the new Congress, as S. 1, the Unfunded Mandate Reform Act of 1995. The Senate Governmental Affairs Committee and Senate Budget Committee held a joint hearing on the bill the following day and it was reported out of the Senate Governmental Affairs Committee with three amendments (9 to 4) on January 9, 1995, and out of the Senate Budget Committee with four amendments (21-0) also on January 9, 1995.

To expedite Senate floor consideration, neither committee filed a committee report. Instead, the committee chairs, Senator William Roth, Jr. on behalf of the Senate Governmental Affairs Committee and Senator Pete Domenici on behalf of the Senate Budget Committee, each submitted a chairman's statement for insertion into the *Congressional Record*.[152] When Senate floor consideration commenced on January 12, 1995, Senator Robert Byrd objected to several features of the way the legislation was being handled, including the absence of a committee report and the pace of consideration. In addition, Senators introduced 228 amendments to the bill. Floor debate lasted for more than two weeks. During floor debate, Senator Kempthorne argued that the bill should be adopted out of a sense of fairness to state and local governments and as a commitment to federalism principles:

> Under this legislation, we are acknowledging for the first time, in a meaningful way, that there must be limits on the Federal Government's propensity to impose costly mandates on other levels of government. As the representatives of those governments have very effectively demonstrated, this is a real problem. Cities, for example, generally are fortunate if they have adequate resources just to meet their own local responsibilities. Unfunded Federal mandates have put a real strain on those resources. This has been the practice of the Federal Government for the past several decades, but in recent years it has mushroomed into an intolerable burden.

This has been due, at least in part, to the Federal Government's own budget crisis. In the past, if Congress felt that a particular problem warranted a national solution, it would often fund that solution with Federal dollars. Mandates imposed on State and local governments could frequently be offset with generous Federal grants. But the Federal Government no longer has the money to fund the governmental actions it wishes to see accomplished throughout the country. In fact, it hasn't had the money to do this for many years. Instead, it borrowed for a long time, to cover those costs. But now the Federal deficit is so large, that the only alternative left for imposing so-called national solutions is to impose unfunded mandates.

... The State legislators and Governors know this. This is why they feel so strongly that legislation regarding this practice must first be in place, before they are asked to ratify a balanced budget amendment. Otherwise, in the drive to achieve a balance Federal budget, Congress might be tempted to mandate that State and local governments shall pick up many of the costs that were formerly Federal. This is why any effort to add a sunset provision to this bill ought to be opposed. Our commitment to protect federalism ought to be permanent.

S. 1 is designed to put in place just such a mechanism. In this regard, it may truly be called balanced legislation. First of all, it helps bring our system of federalism back into balance, by serving as a check against the easy imposition of unfunded mandates. And, second, it does so in a way that strikes a balance between restraining the growth of mandates and recognizing that there may be legitimate exceptions.[153]

Senator Frank Lautenberg was among those opposing UMRA. He argued that the bill should be defeated because, among other things, the federal government has an obligation to set national standards to protect the environment and ensure the quality of life for all Americans:

Halting interstate pollution is an important responsibility of the Federal Government. And I am concerned that this act may have a chilling effect on future Federal environmental legislation. Another issue that may get loss in this debate is the benefit that States and their citizens derive from Federal mandates—even those not fully funded. States may say, we know how best to care for our citizens; a program that may be good for New Jersey, may not be good for Idaho or Ohio. But, I would argue that there is a broader national interest in some very fundamental issues which transcend that premise. I would argue that historically, not all States have provided a floor of satisfactory minimum decency standards for their citizens and that, as a democratic and fair society, we should worry about that. Further, as a practical matter, I would argue that the policies of one State in a society such as ours will certainly affect citizens and taxpayers of another State just as certainly as unfunded mandates can.

Let us look at our welfare system. There has been a lot of discussion about turning welfare over to the States, with few or virtually no Federal guidelines or requirements. What would happen if we do that? Would we see a movement of the disadvantaged between States, putting a heavier burden on the citizens of a State that provides more generous benefits?

Let us look at occupational safety, or environmental regulation. With a patchwork of differing standards across the States, would we see a migration of factories and jobs to States with lower standards? I think so. But by mandating floors in environmental and workplace conditions, the Federal Government ensures that States will comply with minimal standards befitting a complex, interrelated, and decent society.

Or let us look at gun control. My State of New Jersey generally has strong controls on guns. But New Jerseyans still suffer from an epidemic of gun violence – in no small measure because firearms come into New Jersey from other States. Without strong national controls, this will remain a problem. That is why we passed a ban on all assault weapons and why we passed the Brady bill.

Currently the Federal Government discourages a scenario whereby a given State decides not to enforce some worker health and safety laws as a way of lowering costs and attracting industry. A State right next door might feel compelled to lower its standards in order to remain competitive. In the absence of a Federal Standard, we would likely see a bidding war that lowers the quality of life for all Americans.

These are some of a host of very fundamental, very basic, and even profound questions raised by the notion that we should never have unfunded mandates. These are questions each Member of the Senate should consider long and hard, before moving to drastically curtail— or make impossible— any unfunded mandates.[154]

After voting on 44 amendments and several cloture motions, the Senate approved S. 1 on January 27, 1995, 86-10.[155]

One of the amendments approved by the Senate was the "Byrd look-back amendment," which is the only provision in UMRA that allows for the regulation of any mandates based on actual rather than estimated costs. [156] It provided that legislation containing intergovernmental mandates would be considered funded, and hence not subject to a point of order, if it authorized appropriations to cover the estimated direct costs of the intergovernmental mandate and incorporated a prescribed mechanism requiring further review if, in any fiscal year, Congress did not appropriate funds sufficient to cover those costs. Under this mechanism, if the responsible federal agency determines that the appropriation provided was insufficient to cover the estimated direct costs of the mandate it shall notify the appropriate authorizing committees not later than 30 days after the start of the fiscal year and submit recommendations for either implementing a less costly mandate or making the mandate ineffective for the fiscal year. The statutory mechanism must also include expedited procedures for the consideration of legislative recommendations to achieve these outcomes not later than 30 days after the recommendations are submitted to Congress. Finally, the mechanism must provide that the mandate "shall be ineffective until such time as Congress has completed action on the recommendations of the responsible federal agency."[157] After Senator Robert Byrd offered this amendment, the Senate adopted it on January 26, 1995, 100-0.[158]

The House companion bill to S. 1 was H.R. 5, the Unfunded Mandate Reform Act of 1995, which was co-sponsored by Representatives William F. Clinger, Jr., Rob Portman, Gary A. Condit, and Thomas M. Davis. It was reported by the House Government Reform and Oversight Committee, on January 13, 1995, by voice vote and without hearings.[159] Floor consideration began on January 20, 1995. Numerous amendments were introduced by Democratic members to add various exemptions to the bill, such as the health of children and the disabled, the disposal of nuclear waste, and child support enforcement. These amendments were rejected on party-line votes. On February 1, 1995, H.R. 5 was adopted, 360-74, inserted into S. 1 as a House substitute, and sent to conference.[160]

There were two major differences between the House and Senate versions of S. 1. The House version did not include the Byrd look-back amendment, and it permitted judicial review of federal agency compliance with the bill's provisions. Initially, House conferees refused to accept the Byrd look-back amendment and Senate conferees, worried that outside parties could delay regulations for years by filing lawsuits, refused to accept judicial review of federal agency compliance with the bill's provisions. Negotiations continued for six weeks. The deadlock over judicial review was ended by allowing judicial review of whether an appropriate analysis of mandate costs was done, but restricting the court's ability to second-guess the quality of the cost estimates. The deadlock over the Byrd look-back amendment ended when House conferees accepted its inclusion after being assured that its intent was to make certain that Congress, rather than an executive agency, retained responsibility for setting policy.[161]

The Senate adopted the conference report, which renamed the bill the Unfunded Mandates Reform Act of 1995, on March 15, 1995, 91-9, and the

House adopted it the next day, 394-28. President Bill Clinton signed it on March 22, 1995.[162]

End Notes

[1] P.L. 104-4; 109 Stat. 48 *et seq.*; and 2 U.S.C. § 602, 632, 653, 658-658(g), 1501-1504, 1511-1516, 153 1-1538, 1551- 1556, and 1571.

[2] U.S. Advisory Commission on Intergovernmental Relations (ACIR), *Regulatory Federalism: Policy, Process, Impact, and Reform*, A-95 (Washington, DC: ACIR, 1984), pp. 1-18.

[3] Mary McElvenn, "The Federal Impact on Business," *Nation's Business*, vol. 79, no. 1 (January 1991), pp. 23-26; David Warner, "Regulations' Staggering Costs," *Nation's Business*, vol. 80, no. 6 (June 1992), pp. 50-53; Michael Barrier, "Taxing the Man Behind the Tree," *Nation's Business*, vol. 81, no. 9 (September 1993), pp. 31, 32; and Michael Barrier, "Mandates Foes Smell a Victory," *Nation's Business*, vol. 82, no. 9 (September 1994), p. 50.

[4] Senator Dirk Kempthorne, "Unfunded Mandate Reform Act," remarks in the Senate, *Congressional Record*, vol. 141, part 1 (January 12, 1995), p. 1166.

[5] Senator Frank Lautenberg, "Unfunded Mandate Reform Act," remarks in the Senate, *Congressional Record*, vol. 141, part 1 (January 12, 1995), p. 1193.

[6] 2 U.S.C. § 1501.

[7] 2 U.S.C § 658; and 2 U.S.C. § 1532.

[8] 2 U.S.C 658(5)(A), (7)(A) and (10), and 2 U.S.C. § 1503.

[9] 2 U.S.C. § 1551-1553.

[10] ACIR funding was withdrawn following the release for public comment and a hearing on the draft report on federal mandates. ACIR was required by UMRA to conduct the study and to make recommendations for mitigating the effect mandates have on state and local governments. The draft report recommended the elimination of a number of federal mandates which had strong support in Congress. ACIR's commission members decided not to release the report in a party-line vote. Most observers concluded that the draft report was a contributing factor in ACIR's losing its funding. See, John Kincaid, "Review of 'The Politics of Unfunded Mandates: Whither Federalism?' by Paul L. Posner," *Political Science Quarterly*, vol. 114, no. 2 (Summer 1999), pp. 322-323.

[11] 2 U.S.C. § 1571.

[12] U.S. Congress, Senate Committee on Governmental Affairs, *Federal Mandates on State and Local Governments*, 103rd Cong., 1st sess., November 3, 1993, S.Hrg. 103-405 (Washington: GPO, 1994), p. 66.

[13] Catherine H. Lovell, Max Neiman, Robert Kneisel, Adam Rose, and Charles Tobin, *Federal and State Mandating on Local Governments: Report to the National Science Foundation* (Riverside, CA: University of California, June 1979), p. 32.

[14] ACIR, *Regulatory Federalism: Policy, Process, Impact, and Reform*, A-95 (Washington, DC: ACIR, 1984), p. 4.

[15] Ibid. Note: The Supreme Court has emphasized the voluntary nature of federal grant programs and the fact that states and private parties remain free to accept or reject the offer of federal funds and thus avoid the attached conditions. "This Court has repeatedly upheld against constitutional challenge the use of this technique to induce governments and private parties

to cooperate voluntarily with federal policy." Fullilove v. Klutznick, 448 U.S. 448, 474 (1980) (Chief Justice Burger announcing judgment of the Court); see also South Dakota v. Dole, 483 U.S. 203 (1987).

16 Ibid.

17 Ibid., p. 7.

18 Ibid., pp. 7-10.

19 National Conference of State Legislatures, "Unfunded Mandate Principles," Washington, DC, 1994, p. 1 cited in CRS Report 95-62, *Mandates and the Congress*, by Sandra S. Osbourn (out of print, available by request).

20 ACIR, *Federally Induced Costs Affecting State and Local Governments*, M-193 (Washington, DC: ACIR, 1994), p. 3.

21 Ibid., p. 19. Note: ACIR also included laws that expose state and local governments to liability lawsuits, which, at the time, affected such programs as the Superfund toxic wastes cleanup program.

22 Ibid., p. 20.

23 U.S. Congress, Senate Committee on Governmental Affairs, *Federal Mandate Reform Legislation*, 103rd Cong., 2nd sess., April 28, 1994, S.Hrg. 103-1019 (Washington: GPO, 1995), p. 56.

24 Ibid., pp. 53-55, 57-63, 68-70, 162-185, 200-230 and 247-249; U.S. Congress, Senate Committee on Governmental Affairs and Senate Committee on the Budget; U.S. Congress, Senate Committee on Governmental Affairs, *Federal Mandates on State and Local Governments*, 103rd Cong., 1st sess., November 3, 1993, S.Hrg. 103-405 (Washington: GPO, 1994), p. 241-245; and U.S. Congress, Senate Committee on Governmental Affairs, *S. 1 - Unfunded Mandates*, 104th Cong., 1st sess., January 5, 1995, S.Hrg. 104-392 (Washington: GPO, 1995), pp. 90-107.

25 U.S. Government Accountability Office, *Unfunded Mandates: Views Vary About Reform Act's Strengths, Weaknesses, and Options for Improvement*, GAO-05-454, March 31, 2005, pp. 9, 13, 14, http://www.gao.gov/ new.items/d05454.pdf.

26 U.S. Congress, Senate Committee on Governmental Affairs, *Federal Mandate Reform Legislation*, 103rd Cong., 2nd sess., April 28, 1994, S.Hrg. 103-1019 (Washington: GPO, 1995), p. 7.

27 Joseph F. Zimmerman, "National-State Relations: Cooperative Federalism in the Twentieth Century," *Publius: The Journal of Federalism*, vol. 31, no. 2 (Spring 2001), p. 23.

28 ACIR, *Federally Induced Costs Affecting State and Local Governments*, M-193 (Washington, DC: ACIR, 1994), p. 22.

29 Ibid., p. 23.

30 U.S. Government Accountability Office, *Unfunded Mandates: Views Vary About Reform Act's Strengths, Weaknesses, and Options for Improvement*, GAO-05-454, March 31, 2005, pp. 5, 11, 12, 23, 38, 39, 43, 47, 48, http://www.gao.gov/new.items/d05454.pdf.

31 Joseph F. Zimmerman, "Congressional Preemption During the George W. Bush Administration," *Publius: The Journal of Federalism*, vol. 37, no. 3 (Summer 2007), p. 436.

32 U.S. Government Accountability Office, *Unfunded Mandates: Views Vary About Reform Act's Strengths, Weaknesses, and Options for Improvement*, GAO-05-454, March 31, 2005, p. 12, http://www.gao.gov/new.items/ d05454.pdf; and Paul L. Posner, "The Politics of Preemption: Prospects for the States," *PS* (July 2005), p. 372.

33 Paul L. Posner, "Mandates: The Politics of Coercive Federalism," in *Intergovernmental Management for the 21st Century*, eds. Timothy J. Conlan and Paul L. Posner (Washington, DC: Brookings Institution Press, 2008), p. 287; and Paul L. Posner, *The Politics of*

Unfunded Mandates: Whither Federalism? (Washington, DC: Georgetown University Press, 1998), pp. 4, 12-14.

[34] Paul L. Posner, *The Politics of Unfunded Mandates: Whither Federalism?* (Washington, DC: Georgetown University Press, 1998), pp. 12, 13. See also, Joseph F. Zimmerman, "Federally Induced State and Local Government Costs," paper delivered at the 1991 Annual Meeting of the American Political Science Association, Washington, DC, September 1, 1991, p. 4.

[35] U.S. Congress, Senate Committee on Governmental Affairs, *Federal Mandate Reform Legislation*, 103rd Cong., 2nd sess., April 28, 1994, S.Hrg. 103-1019 (Washington: GPO, 1995), p. 11.

[36] National Conference of State Legislatures, "Policy Position on Federal Mandate Relief," effective through August 2011, *http://www.ncsl.org/Default.aspx?TabID=773&tabs=855,20,632#FederalMandate;* and Paul L. Posner, "Mandates: The Politics of Coercive Federalism," in *Intergovernmental Management for the 21st Century*, eds. Timothy J. Conlan and Paul L. Posner (Washington, DC: Brookings Institution Press, 2008), pp. 287, 292, 293.

[37] For further analysis, see CRS Report RL33261, *Internet Taxation: Issues and Legislation*, by Steven Maguire and Nonna A. Noto.

[38] Donald Bruce and William F. Fox, "State and Local Sales Tax Revenue Losses from E-Commerce: Estimates as of July 2004," (Knoxville, TN: University of Tennessee, 2004), p. 5, http://cber.utk.edu/ecomm/Ecom0704.pdf, cited in National Conference of State Legislatures, "Nexus in the New Economy: Ensuring a Level Playing Field for All Commerce," policy position effective through August 2011, *http://www.ncsl.org/Default.aspx?TabID=773&tabs=* 855,20,632#NCSLSupports.

[39] Paul L. Posner, "Mandates: The Politics of Coercive Federalism," in *Intergovernmental Management for the 21st Century*, eds. Timothy J. Conlan and Paul L. Posner (Washington, DC: Brookings Institution Press, 2008), p. 292.

[40] 2 U.S.C. § 658(5)(A).

[41] 2 U.S.C. § 658(5)(B).

[42] 2 U.S.C. § 658(7)(A) and 2 U.S.C. § 658(7)(B).

[43] 2 U.S.C. § 658d(a)(2); Sec. 425 of the Congressional Budget and Impoundment Control Act of 1974, as amended, P.L. 93-344, 88 Stat. 297, 2 U.S.C. § 658 *et seq.*

[44] 2 U.S.C. § 658(5)(B).

[45] U.S. Congress, Senate Committee on Finance, *Work, Opportunity, and Responsibility for Kids Act*, report to accompany H.R. 4737, 107th Cong., 2nd sess., July 25, 2002, S.Rept. 107-221 (Washington: GPO, 2002), p. 61; and 2 U.S.C. § 658(5)(B).

[46] U.S. Congress, Senate Committee on Finance, *Work, Opportunity, and Responsibility for Kids Act*, report to accompany H.R. 4737, 107th Cong., 2nd sess., July 25, 2002, S.Rept. 107-221 (Washington: GPO, 2002), p. 61.

[47] 2 U.S.C. § 658a.

[48] U.S. Congress, Senate Committee on Governmental Affairs, *Unfunded Mandate Reform Act of 1995*, report to accompany S. 1, 104th Cong., 1st sess., January 11, 1995, S.Rept. 104-1 (Washington: GPO, 1995), p. 12.

[49] U.S. General Accounting Office, *Unfunded Mandates: Analysis of Reform Act Coverage*, GAO-04-637, May 12, 2004, pp. 11-17, http://www.gao.gov/new.items/d04637.pdf.

[50] 2 U.S.C. § 602.

[51] 2 U.S.C. § 658b.

[52] 2 U.S.C. § 658c.

[53] 2 U.S.C. § 658 (3)(A)(i).

[54] 2 U.S.C. § 658 (3)(B).

[55] Theresa A. Gullo and Janet M. Kelly, "Federal Unfunded Mandate Reform: A First-Year Retrospective," *Public Administration Review*, vol. 58, no. 5 (September/October 1998), p. 381.

[56] 2 U.S.C. § 658c(a).

[57] 2 U.S.C. § 658d(a); and 2 U.S.C. § 658c(b)(3).

[58] 2 U.S.C. § 658d(c).

[59] 2 U.S.C. § 658e(a); and 2 U.S.C. § 658e(b)(3).

[60] 2 U.S.C. § 658d(d); and 2 U.S.C. § 658d(e).

[61] 2 U.S.C. § 558d(a); Sec. 403(b)(1) of H.Con.Res. 95, adopted April 28, 2005.

[62] 2 U.S.C. § 558d(a). Note: A Senate amendment to S.Con.Res. 13, which was adopted on April 28, 2009, proposed to increase the vote necessary to waive the point of order in the Senate to 60. The amendment was initially agreed to by unanimous consent in the Senate, but was dropped in the final version.

[63] Elizabeth Garrett, "Framework Legislation and Federalism," *Notre Dame Law Review*, vol. 83, no. 4 (2008), p. 1502.

[64] Based on CRS review of the 12 points of order raised in the House, to date, during the 111th Congress.

[65] "Transportation, Treasury, Housing and Urban Development, the Judiciary, the istrict of Columbia, and Independent Agencies Appropriations Act, 2006," proceedings in the Senate, *Congressional Record* (daily ed.) Vol. 151, October 19, 2005, pp. S11526, S11547-S11548.

[66] Senator Robert Corker, "H.R. 3590, the Service Members Home Ownership Tax Act of 2009," remarks in the Senate, *Congressional Record*, daily edition, vol. 155, no. 199 (December 23, 2009), pp. S13803, S13804.

[67] "Consideration of H.R. 3590, the Service Members Home Ownership Tax Act of 2009, Senate Rollcall Vote No. 390," *Congressional Record*, daily edition, vol. 155, no. 199 (December 23, 2009), p. S13831.

[68] "Consideration of H.R. 3590, the Patient Protection and Affordable Care Act, Senate Rollcall Vote No. 396," *Congressional Record*, daily edition, vol. 155, no. 201 (December 24, 2009), p. S13831

[69] U.S. Government Accountability Office, *Unfunded Mandates: Views Vary About Reform Act's Strengths, Weaknesses, and Options for Improvement*, GAO-05-454, March 31, 2005, p. 15, http://www.gao.gov/new.items/ d05454.pdf.

[70] National Conference of State Legislatures, "Policy Position on Federal Mandate Relief," effective through August 2011, *http://www.ncsl.org/Default.aspx?TabID=773&tabs=855,20,632#FederalMandate*

[71] Joint Hearing, U.S. Congress, House Committee on Government Reform, Subcommittee on Energy Policy, Natural Resources and Regulatory Affairs, and House Committee on Rules, Subcommittee on Technology and the House, *Unfunded Mandates: A Five Year Review and Recommendations for Change*, hearing on the Unfunded Mandates Reform Act of 1995, 107th Cong., 1st sess., May 24, 2001, H. Hrg. 107-19 (Washington: GPO, 2001), p. 61.

[72] Paul L. Posner, "Unfunded Mandates Reform Act: 1996 and Beyond," *Publius: The Journal of Federalism*, vol. 27, no. 2 (Spring 1997), pp. 57-59; U.S. General Accounting Office, *Unfunded Mandates: Analysis of Reform Act Coverage*, GAO-04-637, May 12, 2004, p. 19, http://www.gao.gov/new.items/d04637.pdf; and U.S. Government Accountability Office, *Unfunded Mandates: Views Vary About Reform Act's Strengths, Weaknesses, and Options*

for Improvement, GAO-05-454, March 31, 2005, p. 15, *http://www.gao.gov/new.items/ d05454.pdf.*

[73] U.S. Congressional Budget Office, *A Review of CBO's Activities in 2009 Under the Unfunded Mandates Reform Act*, Washington, DC, March 2010, pp. 5, 68, *http://www.cbo.gov/ ftpdocs/104xx/doc10485/03-31-UMRA.pdf.*

[74] Ibid., pp. 47 and 48.

[75] National Conference of State Legislatures, "Policy Position on Federal Mandate Relief," effective through August 2011, *http://www.ncsl.org/Default.aspx?TabID=773&tabs= 855,20,632#FederalMandate*

[76] U.S. Congressional Budget Office, *A Review of CBO's Activities in 2008 Under the Unfunded Mandates Reform Act*, Washington, DC, March 2009, p. 48, *http://www.cbo.gov/ftpdocs/ 100xx/doc10058/03-31-UMRA.pdf;* and U.S. Congressional Budget Office, *A Review of CBO 's Activities in 2009 Under the Unfunded Mandates Reform Act*, Washington, DC, March 2010, p. 4, http://www.cbo.gov/ftpdocs/104xx/doc10485/03-31-UMRA.pdf.

[77] U.S. Congressional Budget Office, *A Review of CBO's Activities in 2009 Under the Unfunded Mandates Reform Act*, Washington, DC, March 2010, pp. 5, 70, *http://www.cbo.gov/ ftpdocs/104xx/doc10485/03-31-UMRA.pdf.*

[78] National Conference of State Legislatures, *Mandate Monitor*, vol. 6, no. 1 (April 8, 2008), p. 1.

[79] NCSL also advocates a revision of the definition of direct costs to capture and more accurately reflect the true costs to state governments of particular federal actions; requiring that mandate statements accompany appropriations bills; enactment of legislation that would require federal reimbursement, as long as the mandate exists, to state and local governments for costs imposed on them by any new federal mandates; restrictions regarding the preemption of state laws; repeal or modification of certain existing mandates; and a review of UMRA's existing exclusions. See, National Conference of State Legislatures, "Policy Position on Federal Mandate Relief," effective through August 2011, http://www.ncsl.org/ Default.aspx?TabID=773&tabs=855,20,632#FederalMandate

[80] U.S. Government Accountability Office, *Unfunded Mandates: Views Vary About Reform Act's Strengths, Weaknesses, and Options for Improvement*, GAO-05-454, March 31, 2005, p. 9, http://www.gao.gov/new.items/ d05454.pdf.

[81] Ibid., p. 12.

[82] Ibid., pp. 9, 13-14.

[83] U.S. Congress, Senate Committee on Government Reform, *S. 389 – The Unfunded Mandates Information Act*, hearing on S. 389, 105th Cong., 2nd sess., June 3, 1998, S.Hrg. 105-664 (Washington: GPO, 1998), pp. 28-35.

[84] U.S. Government Accountability Office, *Unfunded Mandates: Views Vary About Reform Act's Strengths, Weaknesses, and Options for Improvement*, GAO-05-454, March 31, 2005, pp. 22, 23, http://www.gao.gov/new.items/ d05454.pdf. Note: GAO also found that "parties across the sectors suggested that various forms of retrospective analysis are needed for evaluating federal mandates after they are implemented" and "parties in the academic/think tank sector suggested analyzing the benefits of federal mandates, when appropriate, not just costs."

[85] 2 U.S.C. § 1532.

[86] Ibid.

[87] 2 U.S.C. § 1533.

[88] 2 U.S.C. § 1534.

[89] 2 U.S.C. § 1535.

[90] 2 U.S.C. § 1536-1538. Note: Several pilot programs were created by the EPA, including one to provide comprehensive compliance assistance to small communities and another sending faculty from schools of public administration to small communities to "minimize the adverse impact of environmental regulations on small governments." See, U.S. Office of Management and Budget, *Agency Compliance With Title I of the Unfunded Mandates Reform Act of 1995: 4th Annual Report to Congress*, Washington, DC, October 1999, pp. 29-32, http://www.whitehouse.gov/omb/assets and U.S. Office of Management and Budget, *Making Sense of Regulation: 2001 Report to Congress on the Costs and Benefits of Regulations and Unfunded Mandates on State, Local, and Tribal Entities*, Washington, DC, 2001, pp. 186-188, http://www.whitehouse.gov/omb/ assets/omb/inforeg/costbenefitreport.pdf.

[91] U.S. General Accounting Office, *Unfunded Mandates: Reform Act Has Had Little Effect on Agencies' Rulemaking Actions*, GAO-GDD-98-30, February 4, 1998, p. 29, http://www.gao.gov/archive/1998/gg98030.pdf; and U.S. Government Accountability Office, *Unfunded Mandates: Views Vary About Reform Act's Strengths, Weaknesses, and Options for Improvement*, GAO-05-454, March 31, 2005, p. 27, http://www.gao.gov/new.items/d05454.pdf. For further analysis concerning OIRA, see CRS Report RL32397, *Federal Rulemaking: The Role of the Office of Information and Regulatory Affairs*, by Curtis W. Copeland.

[92] U.S. Government Accountability Office, *Unfunded Mandates: Views Vary About Reform Act's Strengths, Weaknesses, and Options for Improvement*, GAO-05-454, March 31, 2005, pp. 26, 27; and U.S. Office of Management and Budget, Office of Information and Regulatory Affairs, *2008 Report to Congress on the Benefits and Costs of Federal Regulations and Unfunded Mandates on State, Local, and Tribal Entities*, Washington, DC, 2008, p. 25.

[93] U.S. General Accounting Office, *Federal Rulemaking: Agencies Often Published Final Actions Without Proposed Rules*, GAO/GGD-98-126, August 31, 1998, pp. 1, 2; and U.S. Government Accountability Office, *Federal Rulemaking: Past Reviews and Emerging Trends Suggest Issues That Merit Congressional Attention*, GAO-06-228T, November 1, 2005, pp. 8-10.

[94] U.S. Government Accountability Office, *Unfunded Mandates: Views Vary About Reform Act's Strengths, Weaknesses, and Options for Improvement*, GAO-05-454, March 31, 2005, p. 27.

[95] 2 U.S. C. § 1532 (a)(2).

[96] U.S. Congress, Senate Committee on Governmental Affairs, *Unfunded Mandate Reform Act of 1995*, report to accompany S. 1, 104th Cong., 1st sess., January 11, 1995, S.Rept. 104-1 (Washington: GPO, 1995), p. 28.

[97] U.S. General Accounting Office, *Unfunded Mandates: Reform Act Has Had Little Effect on Agencies' Rulemaking Actions*, GAO-GDD-98-30, February 4, 1998, p. 16; U.S. Office of Management and Budget, *1997 Report to Congress on the Costs and Benefits of Regulations*, Washington, DC, September 1997, chapter 3; U.S. Office of Management and Budget, *1998 Report to Congress on the Costs and Benefits of Regulations*, Washington, DC, January 1999, p. 44; U.S. Office of Management and Budget, *2000 Report to Congress on the Costs and Benefits of Regulations*, Washington, DC, June 2000, pp. 37, 38; U.S. Office of Management and Budget, *Making Sense of Regulation: 2001 Report to Congress on the Costs and Benefits of Regulations and Unfunded Mandates on State, Local, and Tribal Entities*, Washington, DC, December 2001, pp. 20, 21; U.S. Office of Management and Budget, *Stimulating Smarter Regulation: 2002 Report to Congress on the Costs and Benefits of Regulations and Unfunded Mandates on State, Local, and Tribal Entities*, Washington, DC, December 2002, pp. 46, 47; U.S. Office of Management and Budget,

Informing Regulatory Decisions: 2003Report to Congress on the Costs and Benefits of Regulations and Unfunded Mandates on State, Local, and Tribal Entities, Washington, DC, September 2003, p. 10; U.S. Office of Management and Budget, *Progress in Regulatory Reform: 2004 Report to Congress on the Costs and Benefits of Regulations and Unfunded Mandates on State, Local, and Tribal Entities*, Washington, DC, December 2004, p. 12; U.S. Office of Management and Budget, *Validating Regulatory Analysis: 2005 Report to Congress on the Costs and Benefits of Regulations and Unfunded Mandates on State, Local, and Tribal Entities*, Washington, DC, December 2005, p. 11; U.S. Office of Management and Budget, *2006 Report to Congress on the Costs and Benefits of Regulations and Unfunded Mandates on State, Local, and Tribal Entities*, Washington, DC, January 2007, p. 6; U.S. Office of Management and Budget, *2007 Report to Congress on the Costs and Benefits of Regulations and Unfunded Mandates on State, Local, and Tribal Entities*, Washington, DC, June 2008, p. 7; U.S. Office of Management and Budget, *2008 Report to Congress on the Costs and Benefits of Regulations and Unfunded Mandates on State, Local, and Tribal Entities*, Washington, DC, January 2009, p. 8; U.S. Office of Management and Budget, *Draft 2009 Report to Congress on the Benefits and Costs of Federal Regulations and Unfunded Mandates on State, Local, and Tribal Entities*, Washington, DC, September 21, 2009, p. 8; and U.S. Office of Management and Budget, *2010 Report to Congress on the Benefits and Costs of Federal Regulations and Unfunded Mandates on State, Local, and Tribal Entities*, Washington, DC, July 20, 2010, p. 3.

[98] U.S. Office of Management and Budget, Office of Information and Regulatory Affairs, 2010 Report To Congress On The Benefits And Costs Of Federal Regulations And Unfunded Mandates On State, Local, And Tribal Entities, Washington, DC, July 20, 2010, pp. 77, 78, http://www.whitehouse.gov/sites/default/files/omb/legislative/reports/ 2010_Benefit_Cost_Report.pdf; U.S. Office of Management and Budget, Office of Information and Regulatory Affairs, 2008 Report to Congress on the Benefits and Costs of Federal Regulations and Unfunded Mandates on State, Local, and Tribal Entities, Washington, DC, 2009, pp. 24-27, http://www.whitehouse.gov/omb/assets information_ and_regulatory_affairs/2008_cb_final.pdf; and U.S. Office of Management and Budget, 2000 Report to Congress On the Costs and Benefits of Federal Regulations, Washington, DC, p. 31, http://www.whitehouse.gov/omb/ assets/omb/inforeg/2000fedreg-report.pdf. Notes: The rule on Standards for Privacy of Individually Available Health Information, issued in 2001 by the Department of Health and Human Services, was identified as costing state and local governments $240 million annually, but the rule was later determined not to be an enforceable duty as defined under UMRA. The Department of Homeland Security's (DHS) Chemical Facility Anti-Terrorism Standards Rule, issued in 2007, was identified as having the potential to require certain municipalities that own and/or operate power generating facilities to purchase security enhancements. However, DHS was unable to determine whether the rule would impose an enforceable duty on state and local governments of $100 million or more (adjusted for inflation) in any one year. OMB includes the rule as a state and local government mandate meeting UMRA's requirements "for the sake of completeness."

[99] U.S. General Accounting Office, *Unfunded Mandates: Reform Act Has Had Little Effect on Agencies' Rulemaking Actions*, GAO-GDD-98-30, February 4, 1998, p. 29, *http://www.gao.gov/archive/1998/gg98030.pdf.*

[100] Ibid., pp. 12-16.

[101] Ibid., p. 28.

[102] Ibid., pp. 21, 22.

[103] Joint Hearing, U.S. Congress, House Committee on Government Reform, Subcommittee on Energy Policy, Natural Resources and Regulatory Affairs, and House Committee on Rules, Subcommittee on Technology and the House, *Unfunded Mandates: A Five Year Review and Recommendations for Change*, hearing on the Unfunded Mandates Reform Act of 1995, 107th Cong., 1st sess., May 24, 2001, H. Hrg. 107-19 (Washington: GPO, 2001), p. 40.

[104] Ibid.

[105] U.S. General Accounting Office, *Unfunded Mandates: Analysis of Reform Act Coverage*, GAO-04-637, May 12, 2004, pp. 4, 28-33, http://www.gao.gov/new.items/d04637.pdf.

[106] Ibid., pp. 36, 37.

[107] U.S. Government Accountability Office, *Unfunded Mandates: Views Vary About Reform Act's Strengths, Weaknesses, and Options for Improvement*, GAO-05-454, March 31, 2005, pp. 3, 4, http://www.gao.gov/new.items/ d05454.pdf.

[108] Ibid., p. 20.

[109] U.S. Congress, Senate Committee on Homeland Security and Governmental Affairs, Subcommittee on Oversight of Government Management, the Federal Workforce, and the District of Columbia, *Passing the Buck: A Review of the Unfunded Mandates Reform Act*, hearing on the Unfunded Mandates Reform Act, 109th Cong., 1st sess., April 14, 2005, S. Hrg. 109-82 (Washington: GPO, 2005), p. 52.

[110] Ibid., pp. 16.

[111] Ibid., pp. 22, 23, 27.

[112] Ibid., pp. 112-126, 167-174.

[113] U.S. Office of Management and Budget, *2007 Report to Congress on the Costs and Benefits of Regulations and Unfunded Mandates on State, Local, and Tribal Entities*, Washington, DC, June 2008, p. 16; U.S. Office of Management and Budget, *2008 Report to Congress on the Costs and Benefits of Regulations and Unfunded Mandates on State, Local, and Tribal Entities*, Washington, DC, January 2009, p. 98; and U.S. Office of Management and Budget, *Draft 2009 Report to Congress on the Benefits and Costs of Federal Regulations and Unfunded Mandates on State, Local, and Tribal Entities*, Washington, DC, September 21, 2009, p. 17.

[114] U.S. Congress, Senate Committee on Homeland Security and Governmental Affairs, Subcommittee on Oversight of Government Management, the Federal Workforce, and the District of Columbia, *Passing the Buck: A Review of the Unfunded Mandates Reform Act*, hearing on the Unfunded Mandates Reform Act, 109th Cong., 1st sess., April 14, 2005, S. Hrg. 109-82 (Washington: GPO, 2005), p. 124.

[115] National Conference of State Legislatures, "Policy Position on Federal Mandate Relief," effective through August 2011, *http://www.ncsl.org/Default.aspx?TabID=773&tabs=855,20,632#FederalMandate*

[116] Joint Hearing, U.S. Congress, House Committee on Government Reform, Subcommittee on Energy Policy, Natural Resources and Regulatory Affairs, and House Committee on Rules, Subcommittee on Technology and the House, *Unfunded Mandates: A Five Year Review and Recommendations for Change*, hearing on the Unfunded Mandates Reform Act of 1995, 107th Cong., 1st sess., May 24, 2001, H. Hrg. 107-19 (Washington: GPO, 2001), pp. 80, 88, 89.

[117] U. S. Government Accountability Office, *Unfunded Mandates: Views Vary About Reform Act's Strengths, Weaknesses, and Options for Improvement*, GAO-05-454, March 31, 2005, p. 13, http://www.gao.gov/new.items/ d05454.pdf.

[118] Ibid.

[119] National Conference of State Legislatures, "Policy Position on Federal Mandate Relief," effective through August 2011, *http://www.ncsl.org/Default.aspx?TabID=773&tabs=855,20,632#FederalMandate*

[120] Ibid.

[121] U.S. Office of Management and Budget, *2008 Report to Congress on the Costs and Benefits of Regulations and Unfunded Mandates on State, Local, and Tribal Entities*, Washington, DC, January 2009, p. 76.

[122] U.S. Office of Management and Budget, *Agency Compliance with Title II of the Unfunded Mandates Reform Act of 1995: 4th Annual Report to Congress from the Director of the Office of Management and Budget*, Washington, DC, October 1999, p. 2.

[123] U.S. Office of Management and Budget, *2008 Report to Congress on the Costs and Benefits of Regulations and Unfunded Mandates on State, Local, and Tribal Entities*, Washington, DC, January 2009, pp. 75, 76.

[124] Ibid., p. 133.

[125] President Bill Clinton, "Remarks on Signing the Unfunded Mandates Reform Act of 1995," *Weekly Compilation of Presidential Documents*, vol. 31, no. 12 (March 22, 1995), p. 455.

[126] H.R. 2255, Unfunded Mandates Information and Transparency Act of 2009, has been referred to the House Committees on Oversight and Government Reform (Subcommittee on Commercial and Administrative Law); Rules; Budget; and Judiciary.

[127] H.R. 5818, the Mandate Prevention Act of 2010, has been referred to the House Committees on Rules and Budget.

[128] U.S. Government Accountability Office, *Unfunded Mandates: Views Vary About Reform Act's Strengths, Weaknesses, and Options for Improvement*, GAO-05-454, March 31, 2005, pp. 5-7, 9-14, http://www.gao.gov/ new.items/d05454.pdf.

[129] Robert Pear and David M. Herszenhorn, "Senators Hear Concerns Over Costs of Health Proposal," *The New York Times*, August 6, 2009, http://www.nytimes.com/2009/08/07/ health Clifford Krauss, Governors Fear Added Costs in Health Care Overhaul, *The New York Times*, August 6, 2009, http://www.nytimes.com/ 2009/08/07/business/07medicaid. html;and Chas Sisk, "Tennessee Gov. Bredesen takes lead role in fight over health costs," *The Tennessean*, August 18, 2009, http://www.tennessean.com/article/20090818/NEWS02/ 908180357/1009/ NEWS02/Tennessee+Gov.+Bredesen+takes+lead+role+in+fight+over+health+costs.

[130] U.S. Congressional Budget Office, "Cost Estimate for the Patient Protection and Affordable Care Act," November 18, 2009, p. 18, http://www.cbo.gov/ftpdocs/107xx/doc10731/ Reid_letter_11_18_09.pdf.

[131] Thomas R. Dye, *Understanding Public Policy*, 6th edition (Englewood Cliffs, N.J.: Prentice-Hall, Inc., 1987), p. 301.

[132] Ibid., p. 300; ACIR, *Categorical Grants: Their Role and Design* (Washington, DC: ACIR, 1978), pp. 50-58; and Claude E. Barfield, *Rethinking Federalism: Block Grants and Federal, State, and Local Responsibilities* (Washington, DC: American Enterprise Institute, 1981), pp. 4-8.

[133] Vernon Louviere, "The Strings Become a Noose," *Nation's Business*, vol. 69, no. 3 (March 1981), p. 64; Joan C. Szabo, "How Costly are Mandated Benefits?" *Nation's Business*, vol. 76, no. 4 (April 1988), p. 14; Mary McElvenn, "The Federal Impact on Business," *Nation's Business*, vol. 79, no. 1 (January 1991), pp. 23-26; David Warner, "Regulations' Staggering Costs," *Nation's Business*, vol. 80, no. 6 (June 1992), pp. 50-53; Michael Barrier, "Taxing the Man Behind the Tree," *Nation's Business*, vol. 81, no. 9 (September 1993), pp. 31, 32;

and Michael Barrier, "Mandates Foes Smell a Victory," *Nation's Business*, vol. 82, no. 9 (September 1994), p. 50.

[134] ACIR, *Regulatory Federalism: Policy, Process, Impact, and Reform*, A-95 (Washington, DC: ACIR, 1984), pp. 19- 21; and ACIR, *Federal Regulation of State and Local Governments: The Mixed Record of the 1980s*, A-126 (Washington, DC: ACIR, 1993), pp. 44, 45.

[135] Office of the Vice-President, *Strengthening the Partnership in Intergovernmental Service Delivery, National Performance Review Accompanying Report* (Washington, DC: GPO, September 1993), http://govinfo.library.unt.edu/ npr/library/reports/isd.html.

[136] ACIR, *Regulatory Federalism: Policy, Process, Impact, and Reform*, A-95 (Washington, DC: ACIR, 1984), p. 88.

[137] ACIR, *Federal Regulation of State and Local Governments: The Mixed Record of the 1980s*, A-126 (Washington, DC: ACIR, 1993), p. 61.

[138] Ibid., p. 46; and Timothy J. Conlan and David R. Beam, "Federal Mandates: The Record of Reform and Future Prospects," *Intergovernmental Perspective,* vol. 18, no. 4 (Fall 1992), pp. 9, 10.

[139] Timothy J. Conlan and David R. Beam, "Federal Mandates: The Record of Reform and Future Prospects," *Intergovernmental Perspective,* vol. 18, no. 4 (Fall 1992), pp. 9, 10.

[140] ACIR, *Regulatory Federalism: Policy, Process, Impact, and Reform*, A-95 (Washington, DC: ACIR, 1984), p. 246.

[141] Edward I. Koch, "The Mandate Millstone," *The Public Interest*, no. 61 (Fall 1980), pp. 42-57.

[142] Ibid., p. 42.

[143] Timothy J. Conlan, James D. Riggle, and Donna E. Schwartz, "Deregulating Federalism? The Politics of Mandate Reform in the 104th Congress," *Publius: The Journal of Federalism*, vol. 25, no. 3 (Summer 1995), p. 26; and Jeffrey L. Esser, "National Unfunded Mandates Day: An Idea Whose Time Has Come," *Government Finance Review*, vol. 9, no. 5 (October 1, 1993), p. 3, http://findarticles.com/p/articles/mi_hb6642/is_n5_v9/ai_n28629948/?tag=content;col1.

[144] Timothy J. Conlan, James D. Riggle, and Donna E. Schwartz, "Deregulating Federalism? The Politics of Mandate Reform in the 104th Congress," *Publius: The Journal of Federalism*, vol. 25, no. 3 (Summer 1995), p. 27.

[145] U.S. Congress, Senate Committee on Governmental Affairs, *S. 1 - Unfunded Mandates*, 104th Cong., 1st sess., January 5, 1995, S.Hrg. 104-392 (Washington: GPO, 1995), p. 5.

[146] Mary-Margaret Lamouth, "Local and Congressional Leaders Talk Mandates," *Nation's Cities Weekly*, March 21, 1994, p. 3; Beverly Schlotterbeck, "Rally to Stop the Mandate Madness Galvanizes Anti-mandate Campaign," *County News*, vol. 26, March 21, 1994, pp. 2, 3; and "Cities Gearing Up For National Unfunded Mandates Week," *Illinois Municipal Review* (September 1994), p. 13.

[147] U.S. Congress, Senate Committee on Governmental Affairs, *Unfunded Mandate Reform Act of 1995*, report to accompany S. 1, 104th Cong., 1st sess., January 11, 1995, S.Rept. 104-1 (Washington: GPO, 1995), p. 9.

[148] Ibid.

[149] Timothy J. Conlan, James D. Riggle, and Donna E. Schwartz, "Deregulating Federalism? The Politics of Mandate Reform in the 104th Congress," *Publius: The Journal of Federalism*, vol. 25, no. 3 (Summer 1995), pp. 28-31.

[150] Senator Richard Shelby of Alabama switched from the Democratic to the Republican Party on November 9, 1994, giving the Republican Party a majority of Senate seats.

[151] Representative Newt Gingrich, "Election of Speaker," remarks in the House, *Congressional Record*, vol. 141, part 1 (January 4, 1995), p. H444; Representative Dick Armey, "H. Res.

6, Title 1, Contract With America: A Bill of Accountability," House debate, *Congressional Record*, vol. 141, part 1 (January 4, 1995), pp. H662-H477; and U.S. Congress, House Committee on Ways and Means, *Contract With America - An Overview*, 104th Cong., 1st sess., January 5, 1995 (Washington: GPO, 1995), pp. 11-18.

[152] Senator William Roth, Jr., "Statement of the Chairman on the Reporting By the Governmental Affairs Committee of S. 1, Unfunded Mandate Reform Act of 1995," remarks in the Senate, *Congressional Record*, vol. 141, part 1 (January 9, 1995), pp. 891-898; and Senator Pete Domenici, "Statement of the Senate Committee on the Budget on S. 1, Unfunded Mandate Reform Act of 1995," remarks in the Senate, *Congressional Record*, vol. 141, part 1 (January 11, 1995), pp. 1092-1099.

[153] Senator Dirk Kempthorne, "Unfunded Mandate Reform Act," remarks in the Senate, *Congressional Record*, vol. 141, part 1 (January 12, 1995), p. 1166.

[154] Senator Frank Lautenberg, "Unfunded Mandate Reform Act," remarks in the Senate, *Congressional Record*, vol. 141, part 1 (January 12, 1995), p. 1193.

[155] Timothy J. Conlan, James D. Riggle, and Donna E. Schwartz, "Deregulating Federalism? The Politics of Mandate Reform in the 104th Congress," *Publius: The Journal of Federalism*, vol. 25, no. 3 (Summer 1995), pp. 31, 32; and "Consideration of S. 1, Unfunded Mandate Reform Act, Senate Rollcall Vote No. 61," *Congressional Record*, vol. 141, part 2 (January 27, 1995), pp. 2750, 2751.

[156] Senator Robert Byrd, "Byrd Amendment No. 213," Amendments Submitted, Unfunded Mandate Reform Act of 1995," *Congressional Record*, vol. 141, part 2 (January 24, 1995), p. 2195. See 2 U.S.C. § 658d(a)(B).

[157] Ibid.

[158] "Consideration of S. 1, Unfunded Mandate Reform Act, Senate Rollcall Vote No. 49," *Congressional Record*, vol. 141, part 2 (January 26, 1995), pp. 2606, 2607.

[159] Representative William F. Clinger, Jr., Chair of the House Government Reform and Oversight Committee, indicated in the committee's report that hearings were not necessary because "the Committee held several hearings on this issue as well as on a similar bill last session." Members from the minority party argued in the committee's report that "The haste in which this bill was considered left a number of substantive issues unaddressed, which even the authors conceded at markup that they would like to address on the Floor. Most importantly, a ruling from the Chairman in the middle of the markup prohibited members from offering amendments to the operative sections of Title II and III." U.S. Congress, House Committee on Government Reform and Oversight, *Unfunded Mandate Reform Act of 1995*, report to accompany H.R. 5, 104th Cong., 1st sess., January 13, 1995, H.Rept. 104-1, Part 2 (Washington: GPO, 1995), pp. 53-56. Note: portions of the bill were also sequentially referred to and reported by the Committees on Rules, Budget, and Judiciary.

[160] "Consideration of H.R. 5, Unfunded Mandate Reform Act, House Roll No. 83," *Congressional Record*, vol. 141, part 3 (February 1, 1995), p. 3252, 3258; and Timothy J. Conlan, James D. Riggle, and Donna E. Schwartz, "Deregulating Federalism? The Politics of Mandate Reform in the 104th Congress," *Publius: The Journal of Federalism*, vol. 25, no. 3 (Summer 1995), pp. 33, 34.

[161] Timothy J. Conlan, James D. Riggle, and Donna E. Schwartz, "Deregulating Federalism? The Politics of Mandate Reform in the 104th Congress," *Publius: The Journal of Federalism*, vol. 25, no. 3 (Summer 1995), pp. 36, 37.

[162] "Unfunded Mandate Reform Act of 1995 – Conference Report, Senate Rollcall Vote No. 104," *Congressional Record*, vol. 141, part 6 (March 15, 1995), p. 7876; "Conference Report on S. 1, Unfunded Mandate Reform Act, House Roll No. 252," *Congressional*

Record, vol. 141, part 6 (March 16, 1995), p. 8136; and President Bill Clinton, "Remarks on Signing the Unfunded Mandates Reform Act of 1995," *Weekly Compilation of Presidential Documents*, vol. 31, no. 12 (March 22, 1995), pp. 453-455.

In: Unfunded Mandates Reform Act
Editor: Irene L. DeSilva
ISBN: 978-1-61209-920-0

Chapter 2

A REVIEW OF CBO'S ACTIVITIES IN 2009 UNDER THE UNFUNDED MANDATES REFORM ACT

Congressional Budget Office

The federal government—through laws and regulations—sometimes requires state, local, and tribal governments and various entities in the private sector to expend resources to achieve national goals. In 1995, the Congress passed and the President signed the Unfunded Mandates Reform Act (UMRA) to ensure that, during the legislative process, the Congress receives information about such proposed requirements, known as federal mandates, before enacting a piece of legislation.

UMRA defines a legislative provision as a mandate if that provision, when enacted, would

- Impose an enforceable duty on state, local, or tribal governments or on private-sector entities;[1]
- Reduce or eliminate funding authorized to cover the costs of complying with existing mandates; or
- Increase the stringency of conditions that apply to the distribution of funds through certain mandatory programs or make cuts in federal funding for those programs.

Duties imposed as conditions of federal assistance or requirements tied to participating in voluntary federal programs, such as programs that require entities to have licenses to graze on federal land, generally are not considered mandates as defined in UMRA.

UMRA established procedures for providing information to the Congress about proposed federal mandates. The law requires the Congressional Budget Office (CBO) to prepare mandate statements for bills that are approved by authorizing committees.[2] In those statements, CBO must address whether the direct costs of a bill's federal mandates would be greater than the thresholds established in UMRA and identify any funding that the bill would provide to cover those costs.[3] If the total direct costs of all mandates in the bill exceed the statutory threshold in any of the first five fiscal years in which the mandate is in effect, CBO must provide an estimate of those costs (if feasible) and the basis of its estimate. In 2009, those thresholds, which are adjusted annually for inflation, were $69 million for intergovernmental mandates and $139 million for private-sector mandates.[4] If CBO cannot estimate the cost of a mandate, its statement must indicate that such an estimate is not feasible and explain why.

Direct costs are defined in UMRA as amounts that the private sector or state, local, and tribal governments would be required to spend to comply with the enforceable duty, including amounts that states, localities, and tribes "would be prohibited from raising in revenues." Direct costs exclude amounts that those entities would spend to comply with applicable laws, regulations, or professional standards in effect when the federal mandate is adopted. In addition, such costs are limited to spending that would result directly from the enforceable duty imposed by the legislation rather than from the legislation's broad effects on the economy.

Not all legislation is subject to UMRA's requirements. In enacting that law, the Congress recognized that instances might arise in which budgetary considerations—such as who would bear the costs that a law might impose—should not be a key part of the debate about a legislative proposal. Thus, CBO does not review bills and other legislation that, for example, deal with constitutional or statutory rights, implement international treaty obligations, are necessary for national security, or alter provisions of the Social Security Act related to old-age, survivors', or disability benefits. (For further details, see AppendixA, which outlines UMRA's key provisions as they apply to CBO.)

In addition to the procedures UMRA established for providing information to the Congress, the law also lays out procedural rules for the House of Representatives and the Senate to encourage Members to take information about mandates into account when they consider legislation. Those rules are enforced through the use of points of order. A point of order can be raised in the House or Senate against the consideration of legislation if the committee reporting a bill has not published a statement by CBO on intergovernmental and private-sector mandates. In addition, Members of Congress may raise a point of order against legislation that seeks to impose an intergovernmental mandate whose costs exceed the threshold, unless the legislation authorizes or provides funding to cover those costs. If a point of order is raised under UMRA, each chamber resolves the issue according to its established rules and procedures.

CBO prepares a mandate statement at some point during the legislative process for most of the legislation considered by the Congress. In most cases, that statement is prepared after a committee has approved legislation but before the legislation has been considered on the floor of the House or the Senate. In some instances, though, as noted in the tables in this report, CBO does not review a mandate before its enactment. That situation may occur when legislation is passed without being considered by a committee; when a bill is amended, after CBO's review, on the floor or in conference to include a provision that contains a mandate; or, in some cases, when a mandate is included in one of the appropriation bills, which CBO does not routinely review for mandates under UMRA (because UMRA does not apply to such bills). Also, in some cases, CBO cannot estimate the cost of a mandate—particularly when much of its impact would depend on the nature of the implementing regulations that would be promulgated by federal agencies.

The number of bills or other legislative proposals that contain mandates and the number of individual mandates that appear in proposed legislation generally differ. Because the House and the Senate may consider the same or similar mandates in more than one piece of legislation, the number of bills that contain mandates can exceed the number of individual mandates considered by the Congress in any given year. Conversely, because one bill may contain several mandates, the number of mandates can exceed the number of bills. The tables in this report identify mandates in public laws enacted during calendar year 2009 and in other legislation considered by the Congress in 2009:

- Table 1 on page 4 is a tally of mandates in public laws enacted between 2005 and 2009.
- Table 2 on page 5 is a tally of the mandate statements CBO transmitted between 2005 and 2009.

- Tables 3 and 4 (on pages 6 and 10) list laws enacted in 2009 that contain intergovernmental and private-B sector mandates, respectively.
- Tables 5 and 6 (on pages 16 and 18) list intergovernmental and private-sector mandates, B respectively, that CBO reviewed in 2009 whose costs would exceed UMRA's thresholds or could not be determined.
- Tables 7 and 8 (on pages 23 and 39) list the bills and proposals CBO reviewed in 2009 that contain intergovernmental and private-sector mandates, respectively.

In all cases, the data presented here are for calendar years. (Although data for spending and receipts in the budget are presented in fiscal year terms—from October 1 through September 30—Congressional legislative sessions generally follow the calendar year; thus, data on CBO's cost estimates and mandate statements are presented as calendar year totals.)

Most of the legislation that the Congress considered in 2009 did not contain federal mandates as defined in UMRA. Historically, CBO has reviewed an average of about 580 pieces of legislation per year and identified intergovernmental and private-sector mandates in an average of 13 percent and 16 percent of them, respectively. In 2009, CBO reviewed fewer pieces of legislation (419) and identified about the same number of mandates as in previous years. Therefore, the percentages of bills containing intergovernmental or private-sector mandates in 2009 are slightly higher than the historical averages. Of the bills that CBO reviewed, 17 percent contained intergovernmental mandates and 25 percent contained private-sector mandates (see Tables 7 and 8).

As in previous years, few laws enacted in 2009 contained mandates whose costs, in CBO's estimation, would exceed UMRA's thresholds. Specifically, no laws contained intergovernmental mandates with costs estimated to exceed the threshold, and 14 laws (11 percent of the total enacted) contained private-sector mandates with such costs. Historically, CBO has identified intergovernmental mandates with costs estimated to exceed the threshold in less than 1 percent of public laws and private-sector mandates with such costs in less than 5 percent of public laws. (AppendixB describes those mandates.)

Table 1. Laws Enacted That Contain Mandates, 2005 to 2009.

In 2009, 125 public laws were enacted. Eighteen of those laws contain at least one intergovernmental mandate as defined in the Unfunded Mandates Reform Act, and 26 contain one or more private-sector mandates. A total of 30 intergovernmental mandates and 60 private-sector mandates were enacted. The Congressional Budget Office determined that none of the intergovernmental mandates in those laws have costs that will exceed the statutory threshold of $69 million in 2009, although CBO could not determine the magnitude of the aggregate costs of 3 intergovernmental mandates.

The public laws enacted in 2009 also contain 17 private-sector mandates with annual costs that, in CBO's estimation, will exceed the statutory threshold of $139 million in 2009. CBO could not determine whether costs for 11 private-sector mandates would be above or below the statutory threshold in UMRA.

	2005	2006	2007	2008	2009
	Intergovernmental Mandates				
Laws That Contain Mandates	11	30	14	19	18
Total Mandates Enacted	23	37	20	40	30
Mandates whose costs exceed the statutory threshold	0	2	3	1	0
Mandates whose costs could not be determined	1	2	0	0	3
	Private-Sector Mandates				
Laws That Contain Mandates	19	39	20	29	26
Total Mandates Enacted	30	66	47	64	60
Mandates whose costs exceed the statutory threshold	4	11	10	15	17
Mandates whose costs could not be determined	5	11	8	13	11

Source: Congressional Budget Office.

Note: The thresholds established in UMRA for intergovernmental and private-sector mandates were $50 million and $100 million, respectively, in 1996. CBO has adjusted the statutory thresholds each year for inflation. In 2009, the statutory thresholds for intergovernmental and private-sector mandates were $69 million and $139 million, respectively.

Table 2. Mandate Statements Transmitted by CBO, 2005 to 2009.

The Congressional Budget Office provides mandate statements to the Congress for most of the bills that are reported by authorizing committees and for many other bills and proposed amendments. Most of that legislation is never enacted; of the proposals that are enacted, most contain no federal mandates as defined in the Unfunded Mandates Reform Act.

In 2009, CBO reviewed 419 bills and other legislative proposals. Of those bills and proposals, 70 (about 17 percent) contained intergovernmental mandates and 105 (about 25 percent) contained private-sector mandates. By comparison, the averages for the 2005–2008 period were 15 percent (intergovernmental) and 19 percent (private sector).

Of the bills and proposals CBO analyzed in 2009, 8 (about 2 percent) had intergovernmental mandates with costs greater than the annual threshold of $69 million and 27 (about 6 percent) had private-sector mandates with estimated costs greater than the threshold of $139 million. Both of those figures are higher than the average percentage for the preceding four years. (Tables 7 and 8 on pages 23 and 39 list all of the bills and proposals containing mandates that CBO reviewed in 2009.)

	2005	2006	2007	2008	2009
	Intergovernmental Mandates				
Number of Statements Transmitted	500	478	703	679	419
Number of Statements That Identified Mandates	83	88	111	57	70
Mandate costs of the legislation would exceed the threshold	6	12	5	2	8
CBO could not determine whether mandate costs of the legislation would exceed the threshold	3	3	4	2	12
	Private-Sector Mandates				
Number of Statements Transmitted	500	474	703	679	419
Number of Statements That Identified Mandates	91	93	160	96	105
Mandate costs of the legislation would exceed the threshold	22	23	44	23	27
CBO could not determine whether mandate costs of the legislation would exceed the threshold	11	21	32	17	27

Source: Congressional Budget Office.

Notes: Although not required by law, CBO has completed preliminary reviews and informal estimates for other legislative proposals that are not included in this table.

In some years, CBO prepared more intergovernmental mandate statements than private-sector statements because in some cases the agency was asked to review a specific bill, amendment, or conference report solely for intergovernmental mandates. (In those cases, no private-sector analysis was transmitted to the requesting Member or committee.) A mandate statement may cover more than one mandate; and because the same mandate sometimes appears in multiple bills, a single mandate may be addressed in more than one statement.

Table 3. Laws Enacted in 2009 That Contain Intergovernmental Mandates.

The Congressional Budget Office estimates that most intergovernmental mandates—those that impose duties on state, local, or tribal governments—enacted in 2009 will not impose significant costs on those governments. Only 11 intergovernmental mandates with costs estimated to exceed the annual threshold have been enacted since the Unfunded Mandates Reform Act became effective in 1996. Those mandates are listed in Appendix B.

Of the 125 laws enacted in 2009, 18 contained a total of 30 mandates. In CBO's estimation, none of them have costs that will exceed the threshold under UMRA ($69 million in 2009). For 3 of those mandates, CBO could not determine whether their costs will exceed the threshold. Those mandates are shown in the table in italic type. Mandates with costs estimated to be below the intergovernmental threshold are shown in regular type.

CBO does not review every mandate before enactment. In some cases, legislation is passed without being considered by a committee. Some mandates are included in amendments made on the floor or in conference after CBO's review. In still other cases, mandates can be included in appropriation bills, which CBO generally does not examine for unfunded mandates.

Of the 30 intergovernmental mandates enacted in 2009, CBO reviewed 14 before enactment. The number of mandates CBO did not review is higher than in recent years—about half of those mandates were in appropriation bills in 2009. Of the mandates not reviewed, none are estimated to have a cost above the intergovernmental threshold.

Public Law Number	Title of Legislation	Description of Mandate	Was Mandate Reviewed by CBO Before Enactment?
Laws Containing Intergovernmental Mandates with Aggregate Costs Above the Statutory Threshold			
		None	
Laws Containing Intergovernmental Mandates Whose Aggregate Costs Could Not Be Determined			
111-22	Helping Families Save Their Homes Act of 2009	*Requires entities that acquire foreclosed properties to honor tenants' leases*	Yes
		Prohibits investors in residential mortgages from suing servicers of those loans under some circumstances	Yes
		Preempts state laws that allow individuals to seek compensation from entities that issue the mortgagebacked securities whose modification is protected under the act	Yes

Table 3. (Continued)

Public Law Number	Title of Legislation	Description of Mandate	Was Mandate Reviewed by CBO Before Enactment?
111-68	Continuing Appropriations Resolution, 2010	*Extends existing standards for the security of chemical facilities and requires vulnerability assessments and the development and impleme-ntation of site security plans*	Yes
		Extends some patent and tradem-ark fees through October 31, 2009	No
111-83	Department of Homeland Security Appropriations Act, 2010	*Extends existing standards for the security of chemical facilities and requires vulnerability Asses-ments and the development and Implem-entation of site security plans*	Yes
		Preempts state laws that require governmental entities to pay inter-est rates of less than 17 percent on loans or other financing transactions	No
Laws Containing Intergovernmental Mandates with Aggregate Costs Below the Statutory Threshold			
111-5	American Recovery and Reinvestment Act of 2009	Requires public entities that handle health information to comply with new regulations related to the use, disclosure, and privacy of such information	Yes
		Preempts state standards governing health information	Yes
111-8	Omnibus Appropriations Act, 2009	Requires District of Columbia officials to submit reports to the Congress	No
		Prevents a District of Columbia law—the Legalization of Marij-uana for Medical Treatment Initia-tive of 1998—from taking effect	No
		Increases reporting requirements on state and local governments following chemical releases	No
		Extends some patent and trademark fees through September 30, 2009	No
111-11	Omnibus Public Land Management Act of 2009	Requires a tribal government to enact a water code	No
		Imposes a mandate if the Secretary of the Interior condemns property to implement the water rights settlements	No

Table 3. (Continued)

Public Law Number	Title of Legislation	Description of Mandate	Was Mandate Reviewed by CBO Before Enactment?
111-21	Fraud Enforcement and Recovery Act	Requires public entities, if subpoenaed, to provide evidence or testimony to a new commission	No
111-24	Credit Card Accountability Responsibility and Disclosure Actof 2009	Preempts state laws regarding fees and expiration dates for gift or pre-paid cards that afford consumers less protection than does federal law	No
111-30	Antitrust Criminal Penalty Enhancement and Reform Act of 2004 Extension Act	Preempts state and local laws relating to damages for violations of state or local antitrust laws	No
111-31	Family Smoking Prevention and Tobacco Control Act	Preempts state laws governing tobacco products that are different from or in addition to the federal regulations authorized by the act	Yes
		Requires tobacco manufacturers and distributors of tobacco produ-cts (including tribal governments) to comply with federal regulations relating to the content, labeling, and marketing of tobacco products and to pay fees	Yes
111-32	Supplemental Appropriations Act, 2009	Preempts state laws that require nondepository institutions to charge interest rates of less than 17 percent on loans or other financing transactions	No
111-45	An act to authorize the Dir-ector of the United States Patent and Trademark office to use funds made available under the Trademark Act of 1946 for patent Operations in order to avoid furloughs and reductionsinforce, and for other purposes	Imposes surcharges on patent holders and applicants	No
111-84	National Defense Authorization Act for Fiscal Year 2010	Increases the costs of complying with existing intergovernmental mandates by increasing the numb-er of service members and reserve-ists eligible for protection under the Servicemembers Civil Relief Act	Yes
		Requires public entities, if subpoenaed, to provide evidence or testimony	Yes
111-87	Ryan White HIV/AIDS Treatment Extension Act of 2009	Requires medical facilities to comply with new procedures for notifying emergency response	Yes

Table 3. (Continued)

Public Law Number	Title of Legislation	Description of Mandate	Was Mandate Reviewed by CBO Before Enactment?
		employees of possible exposures to an infectious disease	
111-88	Further Continuing Appropriations Resolution, 2010	Extends some patent and tradem-ark fees through December 18, 2009	No
111-97	Military Spouses Residency Relief Act	Prohibits state and local governm-ents from collecting taxes on an individual's income or personal property, if that individual moved to the jurisdiction to accompany his or her spouse at a military duty station	Yes
111-117	Consolidated Appropria-tions Act, 2010	Extends some patent and tradem-ark fees through September 30, 2010	No
		Requires District of Columbia officials to submit reports to the Congress	No
111-118	Department of Defense Appropriations Act, 2010	Requires copyright holders to participate in a process to set roya-lty rates for certain types of transmissions	Yes

Source: Congressional Budget Office.

Table 4. Laws Enacted in 2009 That Contain Private-Sector Mandates.

Of the 125 public laws enacted last year, 26 contain one or more private-sector mandates, for a total of 60 such mandates enacted in 2009. Fourteen of those 26 laws contained a total of 17 mandates that the Congressional Budget Office estimates will impose costs on the private sector that exceed the annual threshold established in the Unfunded Mandates Reform Act ($139 million in 2009). (Those 17 mandates are shown in the table in bold type.) CBO has identified 84 private-sector mandates enacted since 1996 with costs estimated to exceed the annual threshold (see Appendix B).

The laws enacted in 2009 also contain 11 private-sector mandates whose costs may or may not be above the threshold; CBO could not make a clear determination in those cases. (Those mandates are shown in the table in italic type.) All of the other private-sector mandates enacted in 2009, CBO estimates, will impose costs below the annual threshold. (Those mandates are shown in regular type.)

CBO does not review every mandate before enactment. In some cases, legislation is passed without being considered by a committee. Some mandates are included in amendments made on the floor or in conference after CBO's review. In still other cases, mandates can be included in appropriation bills, which CBO generally does not review for unfunded mandates.

Of the 60 private-sector mandates enacted in 2009, CBO reviewed 28 before enactment. The number of mandates CBO did not not review is higher than in recent years—about half were in appropriation bills. Of the mandates not reviewed, 11 are estimated to have a cost above the private-sector threshold.

Public Law Number	**Title of Legislation**	**Description of Mandate**	**Was Mandate Reviewed by CBO Before Enactment?**
Laws Containing Private-Sector Mandates with Aggregate Costs Above the Statutory Threshold			
111-3	Children's Health Insur-ance Program Reauthoriz-ation Act of 2009	**Increases the rate of the excise tax on tobacco products**	No
		Requires group health plans to permit employees to enroll in the plan if they lose eligibility for Medicaid or the Children's Health Insurance Program or become eligible through those programs for assistance in paying premiums	Yes
		Requires employers to inform employees of potential opportunities to receive assistance in paying premiums	Yes
111-4	DTV Delay Act	**Prohibits the use of the 700 megahertz spectrum by certain owners of the spectrum by extending the deadline for the transition to digital television**	No
111-5	American Recovery and Reinvestment Act of 2009	**Modifies regulations related to limits on the use of certain business losses in unprofitable years following a change in ownership Modifies requirements and conditions of continued health coverage under the Consolidated Omnibus Budget Reconciliation Act (COBRA) for certain employers who offer group health insurance**	Yes[a]
		Authorizes the Secretary of the Treasury to set standards for executive compens-ation by recipients of funds from the Troubled Asset Relief Program	No
		Requires entities to comply with new regulations related to the use, disclosure, and privacy of health information	Yes
111-8	Omnibus Appropriations Act, 2009	**Extends some patent and trademark fees through September 30, 2009**	No
		Makes permanent the authority of the Bureau of Land Management to collect administration fees under the mining law	No

Table 4. (Continued)

Public Law Number	Title of Legislation	Description of Mandate	Was Mandate Reviewed by CBO Before Enactment?
		Increases reporting requirements for certain facilities following chemical releases	No
		Restricts the sales of cluster munitions	No
111-12	Federal Aviation Administration Extension Act of 2009	**Extends excise taxes on aviation fuels and air transportation**	No
111-22	Helping Families Save Their Homes Act of 2009	**Requires depository institutions to pay higher premiums by making permanent the increase in deposit insurance coverage**	Yes
		Requires bank holding companies to pay special assessments	Yes
		Requires entities that acquire foreclosed properties to honor tenants' leases	Yes
		Prohibits investors in residential mortgages from suing servicers of those loans under some circumstances	Yes
		Requires mortgage servicers that engage in certain qualified plans to comply with reporting requirements	Yes
		Requires creditors to provide additional information to borrowers when a mortgage loan is sold or transferred	No
111-24	Credit Card Account-ability Responsibility and Disclosure Act of 2009	**Prohibits issuers of gift cards from collecting certain fees and establishing expiration dates**	Yes
		Places limits on certain fees and interest charges that creditors could collect	Yes
		Restricts the ability of creditors to incre-ase certain rates	Yes
		Prohibits creditors from issuing credit cards to individuals under the age of 21 unless certain requirements are met	Yes
		Imposes several requirements on creditors regarding account payment methods, terms, and disclosures	Yes
111-31	Family Smoking Prevention and Tobacco Control Act	**Imposes a fee on manufacturers and importers of tobacco products to cover the cost to the Food and Drug Adminis-tration of regulating those products**	Yes

Table 4. (Continued)

Public Law Number	Title of Legislation	Description of Mandate	Was Mandate Reviewed by CBO Before Enactment?
		Imposes new requirements related to the labeling and advertising of tobacco products	Yes
		Requires manufacturers and distributors of tobacco products to comply with regulations that establish product standards and regulate the sale, distribution, promotion, and use of tobacco products	Yes
	Federal Retirement Reform Act of 2009	Requires private entities, if subpoenaed, to provide evidence or testimony	No
111-45	An act to authorize the Director of the United States Patent and Trademark Office to use funds made available under the Trademark Act of 1946 for patent operations in order to avoid furloughs and reductions-in-force, and for other purposes	**Imposes surcharges on patent holders and applicants**	No
111-69	Fiscal Year 2010 Federal Aviation Administration Extension Act	**Extends excise taxes on aviation fuels and air transportation**	No
111-92	Worker, Homeownership, and Business Assistance Act of 2009	**Extends the Federal Unemployment Tax Act surtax from December 31, 2009, through June 30, 2011**	No
		Delays implementation of rules for the worldwide allocation of interest	No
		Requires certain preparers of tax returns to file such returns electronically	No
111-116	Fiscal Year 2010 Federal Aviation Administration Extension Act, Part II	**Extends excise taxes on aviation fuels and air transportation**	No
111-117	Consolidated Appropriations Act, 2010	**Extends some patent and trademark fees through September 30, 2010**	No
		Requires Amtrak to allow passengers to put firearms in their checked luggage	No
		Requires certain car manufacturers to inform car dealerships about their rights	No
		Extends the restriction on sales of cluster munitions	No
111-124	An act to extend the Generalized System of	**Extends customs user fees**	No

Table 4. (Continued)

Public Law Number	Title of Legislation	Description of Mandate	Was Mandate Reviewed by CBO Before Enactment?
	Preferences and the Andean Trade Preference Act, and for other purposes		
Laws Containing Private-Sector Mandates Whose Aggregate Costs Could Not Be Determined			
111-68	Continuing Appropriations Resolution, 2010	*Extends existing standards for the security of chemical facilities and requires vulnerability assessments and the development and implementation of site security plans*	Yes
		Extends some patent and trademark fees through October 31, 2009	No
		Extends the restriction on sales of cluster munitions	No
111-73	Enhanced Partnership with Pakistan Actof 2009	*Prohibits the export of major defense equipment toPakistan in the absence of certification and a waiver by the Secretary of State*	Yes
111-83	Department of Homeland Security Appropriations Act, 2010	*Extends existing standards for the security of chemical facilities and requires vulnerability assessments and the development and implementation of site security plans*	Yes
		Authorizes fees for services in the temporary protected status program	No
		Requires any company that collects or retains personal information directly from individuals who participated in the Registered Traveler program to safeguard and dispose of such information in accordance with specified requirements	No
111-84	National Defense Authorization Act for Fiscal Year 2010	*Increases the costs of complying with existing private-sector mandates by increasing the number of service members and reservists eligible for protection under the Servicemembers Civil Relief Act*	Yes
		Requires private entities, if subpoenaed, to provide evidence or testimony	Yes
Laws Containing Private-Sector Mandates with Aggregate Costs Below the Statutory Threshold			
111-11	Omnibus Public Land Management Act of 2009	Imposes a mandate if the Secretary of the Interior condemns property to implement the settlement of water rights	No
111-21	Fraud Enforcement and Recovery Act of 2009	Requires private entities, if subpoenaed, to provide evidence or testimony to a new commission	No

Table 4. (Continued)

Public Law Number	Title of Legislation	Description of Mandate	Was Mandate Reviewed by CBO Before Enactment?
111-30	Antitrust Criminal Penalty Enhancement and Reform Act of 2004 Extension Act	Limits damages that can be recovered by a plaintiff in an antitrust case if the defendant has applied and qualifies for leniency	No
111-42	A joint resolution approving the renewal of import restrictions contained in the Burmese Freedom and Democracy Act of 2003, and for other purposes	Renews the ban on imports from Burma	Yes
		Extends customs user fees	No
111-87	Ryan White HIV/AIDS Treatment Extension Act of 2009	Requires medical facilities to comply with new procedures for notifying emergency response employees of possible exposures to an infectious disease	Yes
111-88	Further Continuing Appropriations Resolution, 2010	Extends some patent and trademark fees through December 18, 2009	No
		Extends the restriction on sales of cluster munitions	No
111-118	Department of Defense Appropriations Act, 2010	Prohibits broadcasters from entering into certain exclusive contracts for the rights to retransmit their programs	Yes
		Requires copyright holders and satellite providers to participate in a process to set royalty rates for certain types of transmissions	Yes
		Extends an authorization for satellite providers to retransmit distant signals to unserved households without obtaining consent or compensating broadcasters	Yes
111-119	Airline Flight Crew Technical Corrections Act	Expands an existing mandate on employers to allow some of their employees to take up to 12 work weeks of unpaid leave for some family and medical reasons	No

Source: Congressional Budget Office.

a. The staff of the Joint Committee on Taxation examines legislative provisions that affect the tax code for federal mandates and estimates their costs. Such information is incorporated into CBO's mandate statements.

Table 5. Intergovernmental Mandates Reviewed by CBO in 2009 Whose Costs Would Exceed the Statutory Threshold or Could Not Be Determined.

In its review of legislation, the Congressional Budget Office identified 6 proposed intergovernmental mandates whose costs would exceed the statutory threshold and another 9 whose costs could not be determined. In some cases, intergovernmentalmandates are identified in more than one bill or piece of legislation, as detailed in Table 7 on page 23. Those mandates or related groups of mandates are listed below with related bill numbers given in parentheses.

Topic	Description of Mandate	Was a Version Enacted into Law in 2009?
Proposed Intergovernmental Mandates with Costs Above the Statutory Threshold		
Climate Change: Carbon Capture and Sequestration Funding	Requires electric utilities to pay assessments, based on the amount of electricity delivered, in order to fu-nd research and technology related to carbon capt-ure and sequestration (H.R. 2454, H.R. 2998, S. 1733)	No
Climate Change: Compliance with Cap-and-Trade Program	Requires publicly owned utilities to participate in a cap-and-trade program to reduce greenhouse gas emissions (H.R. 2454, H.R. 2998, S. 1733)	No
Climate Change: Preemption	Preempts state authority to enforce a cap-and-trade program for greenhouse gases from 2012 through 2017 (H.R. 2454, H.R. 2998, S. 1733)	No
Firefighting Standards	Requires airports to meet new firefighting standards (H.R. 915)	No
Health Care Reform	Places new requirements on state and local govern-ments as employers for offering health care coverage to their employees, establishes new standards for insurance and rating laws, and preempts a number of state laws governing health care coverage (H.R. 3590, with an amendment proposed on November 18, 2009; H.R. 3590, with an amendment incorporating the manager's amendment released on December 19, 2009)	No
Sewage Overflows	Requires publicly owned treatment works to monitor, report, and notify the public, health agencies, and the Environmental Protection Agency about sewer overflows (H.R. 1262, S. 937)	No
Proposed Intergovernmental Mandates Whose Costs Could Not Be Determined		
Chemical Security	Expands and makes permanent existing security requirements on owners and operators of certain chemical facilities and requires high-risk facilities with chemicals to conduct assessments of plans and procedures to reduce the incidence of terrorism (H.R. 2868, Energy and Commerce; H.R. 2868, Homeland Security)	Yes (Public Law 111-68, P.L. 111-83)[a,b]
Climate Change: Standards to	Establishes performance standards for greenhouse gas emissions from new coalfueled power plants and other	No

Table 5. (Continued)

Topic	Description of Mandate	Was a Version Enacted into Law in 2009?
Reduce Green-house Gas Emissions	facilities and authorizes standards for reducing black carbon emissions (H.R. 2454, H.R. 2998, S. 1733)	
Commodity Inv-estment Limits and Transaction Requirements	Imposes limits on investments in certain commodities and places requirements, such as clearing fees, on certain transactions (H.R. 977, H.R. 2454, H.R. 2998, H.R. 3795, Agriculture; H.R. 3795, Financial Serv-ices; H.R. 4173, Introduced; H.R. 4173, Rules)	No
Drinking Water Security	Imposes new security requirements on drinking water facilities (H.R. 3258)	No
Elimination of Existing Rights to Seek Compensation	Prevents investors from seeking damages for contract violations under some circumstances (H.R. 1106)	No
Limits on Swap Investments	Prohibits public entities that invest more than $25 million but less than $50 million from entering into swaps with entities that are not regulated (H.R. 3795, Agriculture; H.R. 3795, Financial Services)	No
Mortgage Finance Requirements	Establishes requirements for creditors, loan origina-tors, mortgage servicers, real estate appraisers, and other entities that participate in the mortgage industry (H.R. 1728; H.R. 4173, Rules)	Yes (One provi-sion in P.L. 111-22)[a,c]
Mortgage Modification	Allows bankruptcy judges to modify the rights of claimholders, including state and local pension funds and housing agencies, by making changes to the terms of home mortgage agreements (H.R. 200, H.R. 1106)	No
Permits for Disch-arges into Waters of the United States	Requires public entities to obtain permits for activities that would affect certain bodies of water (S. 787)	No

Source: Congressional Budget Office.

Note: The mandates in this table were identified by the Congressional Budget Office and the staff of the Joint Committee on Taxation when a bill was reported by an authorizing committee or when CBO was asked to formally review a bill. In some cases, CBO issued more than one formal mandate statement for a topic.

a. The full names of the public laws referred to in this table (ordered by law number) are as follows:

- Public Law 111-22, Helping Families Save Their Homes Act of 2009
- Public Law 111-68, Continuing Appropriations Resolution, 2010
- Public Law 111-83, Department of Homeland Security Appropriations Act, 2010

b. Public Laws 111-68 and 111-83 extended existing regulations related to the security of chemical facilities, although they did not include all of the requirements that CBO reviewed in versions of H.R. 2868.

c. A provision requiring entities that acquire foreclosed properties to honor tenants' leases was enacted in P.L. 111-22.

Table 6. Private-Sector Mandates Reviewed by CBO in 2009 Whose Costs Would Exceed the Statutory Threshold or Could Not Be Determined.

In its review of legislation, the Congressional Budget Office identified 17 proposed private-sector mandates whose costs would exceed the statutory threshold and another 20 whose costs could not be determined. In some cases, private-sector mandates are identified in more than one bill or piece of legislation, as detailed in Table 8 on page 39. Those mandates or related groups of mandates are listed below with related bill numbers given in parentheses.

Topic	Description of Mandate	Was a Version Enacted into Law in 2009?
Proposed Private-Sector Mandates with Costs Above the Statutory Threshold		
Aircraft and Helicopter Standards	Prohibits the operation of certain aircraft that are not in compliance with low-noise standards, requires owners of aircraft to install certain equipment, requires some air carriers to reapply under new standards for antitrust immunity, and requires operators of helicopters and fixed-wing aircraft for emergency medical service to install equipment and adhere to safety procedures (H.R. 915, S. 1451)	No
Climate Change: Carbon Capture and Sequestration Funding	Requires electric utilities to pay assessments, based on the amount of electricity delivered, in order to fund research and technology related to carbon capture and sequestration (H.R. 2454, H.R. 2998, S. 1733)	No
Climate Change: Compliance with Cap-and-Trade Programs	Requires covered facilities to participate in cap-and-trade programs to reduce greenhouse gas emissions (H.R. 2454, H.R. 2998, S. 1733)	No
Consumer Financial Protection	Requires nondepository entities to pay fees to a new regulatory agency and requires financial companies to register with the agency, provide whistleblower protection for their employees, meet standards for sales practices and examinations, and comply with reporting requirements (H.R. 3126; H.R. 4173, Introduced; H.R. 4173, Rules)	No
Credit Card Regulation	Prevents creditors and issuers of gift cards from imposing certain fees and requires creditors to comply with transaction and reporting requirements (H.R. 627, H.R. 3639, S. 414)	Yes (Public Law 111-24)[a]
Data Security	Requires entities to establish security systems to monitor access to personal information and requires information brokers and other entities to comply with Disclosure and reporting requirements (H.R. 2221, S. 1490)	No
Energy Conservation Standards	Establishes energy conservation standards for appliances and lighting products (H.R. 2454, H.R. 2998, S. 1462)[b]	No

Table 6. (Continued)

Topic	Description of Mandate	Was a Version Enacted into Law in 2009?
Federal Deposit Insurance Fees	Requires depository institutions to pay higher premiums by making permanent the increase in deposit	Yes (P.L. 111-22)[a]
Financial Markets	Requires large financial institutions to pay fees to the regulatory agency; creates a fiduciary duty for certain broker dealers; and imposes requirements for prudential standards, reporting, and planning on entities that engage in financial activities (H.R. 4173, Introduced; H.R. 4173, Rules)	No
Food Safety	Requires entities that manufacture, process, pack, or hold food to register with the Department of Health and Human Services, pay an annual fee, and comply with safety standards and new procedures for recordkeeping and tracking of food (H.R. 2749)	No
Health Care Reform	Requires individuals to obtain health insurance coverage, places new requirements on employers for offering health care coverage to their employees, and imposes other requirements related to nutrition labeling and health information (H.R. 3590, with an amendment proposed on November 18, 2009; H.R. 3590, with an amendment incorporating the manager's amendment released on December 19, 2009; H.R. 3962, with an amendment from November 3, 2009; H.R. 3962, with an amendment from November 3, 2009, and updated to reflect enactment of H.R. 3548)	No
Insurance Coverage	Modifies the requirements and conditions of continued health insurance coverage under the Consolidated Omnibus Budget Reconciliation Act (COBRA) for certain employers who offer group health insurance (H.R. 1; H.R. 1, with an amendment; H.R. 3962, with an amendment from November 3, 2009; H.R. 3962, with an amendment from November 3, 2009, and updated to reflect enactment of H.R. 3548)	Yes (P.L. 111-5)[a]
Passport Fees	Makes permanent the authority of the Secretary of State to collect a surcharge on passport applications (H.R. 2410)	No
Patent Infringement Claims	Places limits on certain agreements between drug manufacturers for settling patent infringement claims (H.R. 3962, with an amendment from November 3, 2009; H.R. 3962, with an amendment from November 3, 2009, and updated to reflect enactment of H.R. 3548)	No
Revenue-Raising Provisions: Decrease in Offsets to Taxable Income	Modifies regulations related to limitations on the use of certain business losses in unprofitable years following a change in ownership (H.R. 1; H.R. 1, with an Amendment)[c]	Yes (P.L. 111-5)[a]
Revenue-Raising Provisions: Surcharge on High-Income Individuals	Imposes an income tax surcharge on high-income individuals (H.R. 3962, with an amendment from November 3, 2009; H.R. 3962, with an amendment from November 3, 2009, and updated to	No

Table 6. (Continued)

Topic	Description of Mandate	Was a Version Enacted into Law in 2009?
	reflect enactment of H.R. 3548)[c]	
Tobacco Products Regulation	Imposes a fee on manufacturers and importers of tobacco products and imposes new requirements related to the labeling and advertising of tobacco products (H.R. 1256, Energy and Commerce; H.R. 1256, Oversight and Government Reform; H.R. 1256, as passed by the House; S. 982)	Yes (P.L. 111-31)[a]
Airline Pilot Training	Requires air carriers to hire pilots who have a certain level of experience and to develop safety programs for pilots, including training and a mentoring program (H.R. 3371)	No
Ban on Defense Exports to Pakistan	Prohibits the export of defense equipment to Pakistan in the absence of certification and a waiver by the Secretary of State (S. 962)	Yes (P.L. 111-73)[a]
Building Code Updates	Requires private entities to comply with new energy-efficiency standards in state and local building codes (S. 1733)	No
Chemical Security	Expands and makes permanent existing security requ-irements on owners and operators of certain chemical facilities and requires high-risk facilities with Chemi-cals to conduct assessments of plans and procedures to reduce the incidence of terrorism (H.R. 2868, Energy and Commerce; H.R. 2868, Homeland Security)	Yes (P.L. 111-68, P.L. 111-83)[a,d]
Climate Change: Standards to Reduce Greenho-use Gas Emissions	Establishes standards for greenhouse gas emissions from new coal-fueled power plants and other sources and authorizes standards for reducing black carbon emissions (H.R. 2454, H.R. 2998, S. 1733)	No
Commodity Investment Limits and Transaction Requirements	Imposes limits on investments in certain commodities and places requirements, such as clearing fees, on certain transactions (H.R. 977; H.R. 2454; H.R. 2998; H.R 3795, Agriculture; H.R. 3795, Financial Services; H.R. 4173, Introduced; H.R. 4173, Rules)	No
Compensation Limits	Restricts compensation for individuals at financial institutions (H.R. 1575; H.R. 1664; H.R. 3269; H.R. 4173, Introduced; H.R. 4173, Rules)	No
Development of Electric Infrastru-cture	Requires owners and operators of electric infrastructure to comply with cybersecurity rules and gives the Federal Energy Regulatory Commission the authority to use eminent domain to acquire rights-of-way for new transmission projects (H.R. 2998, S. 1462)	No
Elimination of an Existing Right to Seek Compens-ation	Prevents investors from seeking damages for contract violations under some circumstances (H.R. 1106)	No
Maritime Safety Requirements	Establishes new safety requirements for commercial and recreational vessels (H.R. 2652, H.R. 3619, S. 1194)	No

Table 6. (Continued)

Topic	Description of Mandate	Was a Version Enacted into Law in 2009?
Mortgage Finance Requirements	Establishes requirements for creditors, loan originators, mortgage servicers, real estate appraisers, and other entities that participate in the mortgage industry (H.R. 1728; H.R. 4173, Rules)	Yes (One provision in P.L. 111-22)[a,e]
Mortgage Modification	Allows bankruptcy judges to modify the rights of claimholders by making changes to the terms of home mortgage agreements (H.R. 200, H.R. 1106)	No
Oil Spill Prevention	Requires merchant mariners to comply with new medical standards established by the U.S. Coast Guard (S. 685)	No
Pension Plans	Requires service providers of defined-contribution retirement plans subject to the Employee Retirement Income Security Act of 1974 (ERISA) and certain plan administrators to provide information, prohibits providers of investment services to definedcontribution retirement plans subject to ERISA from supplying investment advice to those plans, and imposes requirements on other service providers that supply investment advice to plans (H.R. 2989)	No
Permits for Discharges into Waters of the United States	Requires private entities to obtain permits for activities that would affect certain bodies of water (S. 787)	No
Protection for Service Members	Increases the costs of complying with existing private-sector mandates by increasing the number of service members and reservists eligible for protection under the Servicemembers Civil Relief Act (H.R. 2647, S. 1390)[f]	Yes (P.L. 111-84)[a]
Radioactive Waste	Prohibits the import of low-level radioactive waste (H.R. 515)	No
Railroad Antitrust Regulations	Subjects railroad carriers to certain antitrust statutes (H.R. 233, S. 146)	No
Royalties for Performances	Requires over-the-air broadcasters to pay new royalty fees to holders of copyrights on sound recordings (H.R. 848)	No
Sanctions Against Iran	Bans all imports from and some exports to Iran, extends and expands sanctions under the Iran Sanctions Act, imposes new license requirements on exporters of certain products, and freezes the assets of family members and certain associates of Iranian government officials subject to sanctions (H.R. 2194, S. 2799)	No

Source: Congressional Budget Office.

Note: The mandates in this table were identified by the Congressional Budget Office and the staff of the Joint Committee on Taxation when a bill was reported by an authorizing committee or when CBO was asked to formally review a bill. In some cases, CBO issued more than one formal mandate statement for a topic.

a. The full names of the public laws referred to in this table (ordered by law number) are as follows:
   - Public Law 111-5, American Recovery and Reinvestment Act of 2009
   - Public Law 111-22, Helping Families Save Their Homes Act of 2009
   - Public Law 111-24, Credit Card Accountability Responsibility and Disclosure Act of 2009
   - Public Law 111-31, Family Smoking Prevention and Tobacco Control Act
   - Public Law 111-68, Continuing Appropriations Resolution, 2010
   - Public Law 111-73, Enhanced Partnership with Pakistan Act of 2009
   - Public Law 111-83, Department of Homeland Security Appropriations Act, 2010
   - Public Law 111-84, National Defense Authorization Act for Fiscal Year 2010

b. CBO determined that the aggregate cost of the energy conservation standards in H.R. 2454 and H.R. 2998 would exceed the annual threshold established in the Unfunded Mandates Reform Act (UMRA). S. 1462 contains many of the standards included in H.R. 2454 and H.R. 2998, but CBO could not determine whether the aggregate cost of the mandates in S. 1462 would exceed the annual threshold.

c. The staff of the Joint Committee on Taxation examines legislative provisions affecting the tax code to identify federal mandates and estimate their costs. Such information is incorporated into CBO's mandate statements.

d. Public Laws 111-68 and 111-83 extended existing regulations related to the security of chemical facilities, although they did not include all of the requirements that CBO reviewed in versions of H.R. 2868.

e. A provision requiring entities that acquire foreclosed properties to honor tenants' leases was enacted in P.L. 111-22.

f. The Servicemembers Civil Relief Act provides benefits and protection to active-duty service members and reservists, including the right to maintain a single state of residence for purposes of state and local personal income taxes and the right to request a deferral in the payment of certain state and local taxes and fees. The act also requires creditors to reduce the interest rate on service members' loan obligations to 6 percent when the acquisition of such obligations predates active-duty service; allows courts to temporarily stay certain civil proceedings, such as evictions, foreclosures, and repossessions; and precludes the use of a service member's personal assets to satisfy the member's trade or business liability while he or she is in military service.

Table 7. Bills Reviewed by CBO in 2009 That Contain Intergovernmental Mandates.

Of the 419 bills or legislative proposals that the Congressional Budget Office reviewed in 2009 for mandates as defined in the Unfunded Mandates Reform Act, 70 contained intergovernmental mandates. Of those 70 bills, 8 contained mandates with aggregate costs that CBO estimated would exceed the statutory threshold in UMRA ($69 million in 2009). Some bills were considered by more than one committee; in those cases, the table lists the various versions of the bill.
Bills containing intergovernmental mandates whose aggregate costs are estimated to exceed the threshold are listed first in the table. Mandates with costs above the statutory threshold are shown in bold type, mandates with uncertain costs are in italic type, and mandates with costs below the threshold are in regular type.

Bill Number (Committee or status)	Title of Legislation	Description of Mandate
Bills Containing Intergovernmental Mandates with Aggregate Costs Above the Statutory Threshold[a]		
H.R. 915	FAA Reauthorization Act of 2009	**Requires airports to meet new firefighting standards** Requires airports to submit contingency plans for emergency circumstances Requires airports to use a qualifications-based system when awarding contracts financed with passenger facility charges Requires states to allow the Federal Aviation Administration access to criminal history records
H.R. 1262	Water Quality Investment Act of 2009	**Requires publicly owned treatment works to monitor, report, and notify the public, health agencies, and the Environmental Protection Agency about sewer Overflows**
H.R. 2454	American Clean Energy and Security Act of 2009	**Requires publicly owned utilities to participate in a cap-and-trade program to reduce greenhouse gas emissions** **Preempts state authority to enforce a cap-and-trade program to reduce greenhouse gas emissions from 2012 through 2017**
		Requires electric utilities to pay assessments based on the amount of electricity delivered to retail customers
		Establishes performance standards for new coal-fueled power plants and facilities not covered by the cap-and-trade program and authorizes standards for reducing black carbon emissions *Imposes position limits, trans-action fees, and reporting requirements on participants in certain commodities markets*
		Requires electric utilities to certify that a minimum percentage of their sales comes from renewable sources
		Creates reporting and planning requirements for entities that produce greenhouse gas emissions
		Requires state regulatory agencies to consider energy-related standards

Table 7. (Continued)

Bill Number (Committee or status)	Title of Legislation	Description of Mandate
		Requires the District of Columbia to purchase water-efficient products and services
		Authorizes the Department of Energy to revise the list of vehicles that states can procure for their fleets
		Preempts state laws relating to energy efficiency
		Preempts state laws relating to the production and importation of hydrofluorocarbons
H.R. 2998	American Clean Energy and Security Act	**Requires publicly owned utilities to participate in a cap-and-trade program to reduce greenhouse gas emissions Preempts state authority to enforce a cap-and-trade program to reduce greenhouse gas emissions from 2012 through 2017**
		Requires electric utilities to pay assessments based on the amount of electricity delivered to retail customers
		Establishes performance standards for new coal-fueled power plants and facilities not covered by the cap-and-trade program and authorizes standards for reducing black carbon emissions
		Imposes position limits, transaction fees, and reporting requirements on participants in certain commodities markets
		Requires electric utilities to certify that a minimum percentage of their sales comes from renewable sources
		Creates reporting and planning requirements for entities that produce greenhouse gas emissions
		Requires state regulatory agencies to consider energy-related standards
		Requires the District of Columbia to purchase water-efficient products and services
		Authorizes the Department of Energy to revise the list of vehicles that states can procure for their fleets
		Requires public entities, if subpoenaed, to provide evidence or testimony
		Imposes a mandate if the Federal Energy Regulatory Commi-ssion (FERC) uses eminent domain to acquire rights-of- way for new transmission projects
		Preempts state law by authorizing FERC to issue construc-tion permits for transmission projects when a state has rejected a request for a permit
		Preempts state laws relating to energy efficiency Preempts state laws relating to the production and importation of hydrofluorocarbons
H.R. 3590	Patient Protec-tion and Affor-dable Care Act (Amend-ment	**Requires state and local governments as employers to comply with new and existing standards regarding health insurance coverage**

Table 7. (Continued)

Bill Number (Committee or status)	Title of Legislation	Description of Mandate
	in the nature of a substitute proposed in the Senate on November 18, 2009)	Requires public and private entities that handle health information to comply with new regulations
		Requires states to reimburse the federal government for any net increase in federal costs resulting from mandatory health insurance benefits established or maintained by the state
		Requires states to assess a charge on or provide payments to health plans and issuers of health insurance if the actuarial risk of the enrollees of such plans does not meet standards established in the bill
		Requires public and private hospitals operating in the United States to establish, update, and make public a list of standard Charges for items and services provided by the hospital
		Requires public and private owners and operators of vending machines to comply with standards for nutrition labeling
		Requires states to ensure that issuers of health insurance Com-ply with new standards governing the percentage of total Pre-mium revenues that must be expended on health care coverage
		Requires states to adopt uniform rating standards for all health plans in each insurance market
		Requires states to enact laws if they wish to prohibit
		exchanges from offering a community health insurance option or if they choose to prohibit nationwide plans
		Preempts state laws governing health insurance, including laws that establish standards for benefits and coverage and laws that regulate risk pools
		Preempts state or local laws that require the disclosure of the nutritional content of food offered for sale by restaurants, retail food establishments, and operators of vending machines if the requirements in those laws are not similar to the ones in the bill
		Preempts state laws that provide greater protection for nursing mothers than does the bill Preempts state and local laws that require manufacturers of a drug, device, biological, or medical supply covered by the bill to disclose or report a payment or other transfer of value provided to a physician or teaching hospital
		Requires state and local governments as employers to comply with new and existing standards regarding health insurance coverage
		Requires public and private entities that handle health information to comply with new regulations related to the financial and administrative transactions of such information
		Requires states to reimburse the federal government for any net increase in federal costs resulting from mandatory health insurance benefits established or maintained by the state

Table 7. (Continued)

Bill Number (Committee or status)	Title of Legislation	Description of Mandate
		Requires states to assess a charge on or provide payments to health plans and issuers of health insurance if the actuarial risk of the enrollees of such plans does not meet standards established in the bill
		Requires public and private hospitals operating in the United States to establish, update, and make public a list of standard Charges for items and services provided by the hospital
		Requires public and private owners and operators of vending machines to comply with standards for nutrition labeling
		Requires states to adopt uniform rating standards for all health plans in each insurance market
		Preempts state laws governing health insurance, including laws that establish standards for benefits and coverage and laws that regulate risk pools
		Preempts state or local laws that require the disclosure of the nutritional content of food offered for sale by restaurants, retail food establishments, and operators of vending machines if those laws are not similar to those required under the bill
		Preempts state laws that provide greater protection for nursing mothers than does the bill
		Preempts state and local laws that require manufacturers of a drug, device, biological, or medical supply covered by the bill to disclose or report a payment or other transfer of value provided to a physician or teaching hospital
		Preempts state licensing laws in cases in which a health care professional is licensed in one state but provides services in another state under a contract or compact with a tribal health program
S. 937	Sewage Overflow Community Right-to-Know Act	**Requires publicly owned treatment works to monitor, report, and notify the public, health agencies, and the Environmental Protection Agency about sewer overflows**
S. 1733	Clean Energy Jobs and American Power Act	**Requires publicly owned utilities to participate in a cap-and-trade program to reduce greenhouse gas emissions**
		Preempts state authority to enforce a cap-and-trade program to reduce greenhouse gas emissions from 2012 through 2017
		Requires electric utilities to pay assessments based on the amount of electricity delivered to retail customers
		Establishes performance standards for new coal-fueled power plants and geological storage of carbon dioxide and authorizes standards for black carbon emissions
		Creates reporting requirements for entities that produce greenhouse gas emissions
		Requires public entities to implement and enforce new energy-efficiency standards in building codes

Table 7. (Continued)

Bill Number (Committee or status)	Title of Legislation	Description of Mandate
		Requires the District of Columbia to purchase water-efficient products and services
		Preempts state laws relating to the production and importation of hydrofluorocarbons
Bills Containing Intergovernmental Mandates Whose Aggregate Costs Could Not Be Determined		
H.R. 200	Helping Families Save Their Homes in Bankruptcy Act of 2009	*Allows bankruptcy judges to modify the rights of claimholders, including state and local pension funds and housing agencies, by making changes to the terms of home mortgage agreements*
		Requires mortgage claimholders to file timely notice with the court before adding fees, costs, or charges while a bankruptcy case is pending
H.R. 977	Derivatives Markets Trans-parency and Accoun-tability Act of 2009	*Imposes position limits, transaction fees, and reporting requirements on pension funds and public utilities*
H.R. 1106	Helping Families Save Their Homes Act of 2009	*Allows bankruptcy judges to modify the rights of claimholders, including state and local pension funds and housing agencies, by making changes to the terms of home mortgage agreements*
		Prevents investors from seeking damages for contract violations under some circumstances
		Prevents investors in residential mortgages from suing servicers of those loans under some circumstances
		Requires mortgage servicers to provide reports about mortgages
H.R. 1728	Mortgage Reform and Anti-Predatory Lending Act	*Requires securitizers to ensure that mortgage debtors are able to make their mortgage payments*
		Requires entities that acquire foreclosed properties to honor tenants' leases
		Preempts state property and securities laws
H.R. 2868 (Energy and Commerce)	Chemical Facility Anti-Terrorism Act of 2009	*Expands and makes permanent existing security require-ments on owners and operators of certain chemical facilities*
		Requires high-risk public facilities with chemicals to conduct assessments of plans and procedures to reduce the incidence of terrorism
		Provides whistle-blower protection to employees of chemical facilities
		Preempts state and local disclosure laws
H.R. 2868 (Homeland Security)	Chemical Facility Anti-Terrorism Act of 2009	*Expands and makes permanent existing security requirem-ents On owners and operators of certain chemical facilities*

Table 7. (Continued)

Bill Number (Committee or status)	Title of Legislation	Description of Mandate
		Requires high-risk public facilities with chemicals to conduct assessments of plans and procedures to reduce the incidence of terrorism
		Provides whistle-blower protection to employees of chemical facilities
		Preempts state and local disclosure laws
H.R. 3258	Drinking Water System Security Act of 2009	*Imposes new security requirements on drinking water facilities*
		Preempts state and local laws governing public access to information and drinking water security
H.R. 3795 (Financial Services)	Over-the-Counter Derivatives Markets Act of 2009	*Imposes position limits, transaction fees, and reporting requirements on public entities that participate in swaps*
		Prohibits public entities that invest more than $25 million but less than $50 million from entering into swaps with entities that are not regulated
		Preempts state laws that affect swaps
H.R. 4173 (Introduced)	Wall Street Reform and Consumer Protection Act of 2009	*Imposes position limits, transaction fees, and reporting requirements on public entities that participate in swaps*
		Requires housing finance and student loan agencies to register with the Consumer Financial Protection Agency, provide whistle-blower protection for their employees, meet standards for sales practices and examinations, comply with reporting requirements, and pay fees
		Imposes requirements for prudential standards, reporting, and planning on entities that engage in financial activities
		Prohibits states from increasing the fees they levy on depository institutions for purposes of ensuring consumer compliance
		Preempts state laws that affect swaps, insurance, and consumer protection
H.R. 4173 (Rules)	Wall Street Ref-orm and Consu-mer Protection Act of 2009	*Imposes position limits, transaction fees, and reporting requirements on public entities that participate in swaps*
		Requires securitizers to ensure that mortgage debtors are able to make their mortgage payments
		Prohibits creditors from charging some fees and from issuing some types of mortgages
		Requires creditors to provide additional disclosures to mortgage debtors, establish escrow accounts for some mortgages, and get an appraisal of a property that would secure a subprime loan
		Requires housing finance and student loan agencies to register with the Consumer Financial Protection Agency, provide whistle- blower protection for their employees, meet standards for sales practices and examinations, comply with reporting requirements, and pay fees
		Imposes requirements for prudential standards, reporting, and planning on entities that engage in financial activities

Table 7. (Continued)

Bill Number (Committee or status)	Title of Legislation	Description of Mandate
		Prohibits mortgage servicers, under some circumstances, from obtaining hazard insurance on behalf of debtors and charging them for the costs of the insurance and other fees
		Prohibits states from increasing the fees they levy on depository institutions for purposes of ensuring consumer compliance Preempts state laws that affect swaps, insurance, and consumers
S. 787	Clean Water Restoration Act	*Requires public entities to obtain permits for activities that would affect certain bodies of water*
H.R. 1	American Recovery and Reinvestment Act of 2009	Requires public entities to comply with new regulations related to the use, disclosure, and privacy of health information Preempts state standards governing health information
H.R. 1	American recovery and Reinvestment Act of 2009 (Amendment in the nature of a substitute, as introduced by Senators Inouye and Baucus on January 31, 2009)	Requires public entities to comply with new regulations related to the use, disclosure, and privacy of health information
		Preempts state standards governing health information
H.R. 42	Commission on Wartime Relocation and Internment of Latin Americans of Japanese Descent Act	Requires public entities, if subpoenaed, to provide evidence or testimony
H.R. 157	District of Columbia House Voting Rights Act of 2009	Preempts state laws governing elections
H.R. 384	TARP Reform and Accountability Act	Preempts state antitrust laws Prohibits investors in residential mortgages from suing servicers of those loans under some circumstances
H.R. 466	Wounded Veteran Job Security Act	Requires state, local, and tribal governments as employers to retain certain employees and grant them seniority and other rights and benefits
H.R. 788	A bill to provide a safe harbor for mortgage servicers who engage in specified	Prohibits investors in residential mortgages from suing servicers of those loans under some circumstances
		Preempts state laws that protect investors
		Imposes reporting requirements on mortgage servicers

Table 7. (Continued)

Bill Number (Committee or status)	Title of Legislation	Description of Mandate
	mortgage loan modifications, and for other purposes	
H.R. 848	Performance Rights Act	Requires publicly owned radio stations to pay new royalty fees to holders of copyrights on sound recordings
H.R. 860	Coral Reef Co-nservation Act Reauthoriz-ation and Enh-ancement Am-endments of 2009	Requires public entities to obtain permits for activities that could affect coral reefs
H.R. 911	Stop Child Ab-use in Reside-ntial Programs for Te-ens Act of 2009	Requires public entities to comply with new training and disclosure requirements
		Requires public entities to comply with minimum health and safety standards for operating residential programs
H.R. 1065	White Moun-tain Apache Tribe Water Rights Quant-ification Act of 2009	Requires the tribe to enact a water code Prohibits the tribe from objecting to the drilling or use of some wells
H.R. 1084	Commercial Advertisement Loudness Miti-gation (CALM) Act	Imposes limits on sound volume for broadcasters and providers of video, satellite, and cable services
H.R. 1256 (As passed by the House)	Family Smok-ing Prevention and Tobacco Control Act	Preempts certain state laws governing tobacco products
		Imposes fees on tribal governments that manufacture or distribute tobacco products
		Imposes new requirements related to the labeling and advertising of tobacco products
		Requires manufacturers and distributors of tobacco products to comply with regulations that establish product standards and that regulate the sale, distribution, promotion, and use of tobacco products
H.R. 1256 (Energy and Commerce)	Family Smok-ing Prevention and Tobacco Control Act	Preempts certain state laws governing tobacco products
		Imposes fees on tribal governments that manufacture or distribute tobacco products
		Imposes new requirements related to the labeling and advertising of tobacco products
		Requires manufacturers and distributors of tobacco products to comply with regulations that establish product standards and that regulate the sale, distribution, promotion, and use of tobacco products

Table 7. (Continued)

Bill Number (Committee or status)	Title of Legislation	Description of Mandate
H.R. 1256 (Oversight Reform) and Government	Family Smoking Prevention and Tobacco Control Act	Preempts certain state laws governing tobacco products
		Imposes fees on tribal governments that manufacture or distribute tobacco products
		Imposes new requirements related to the labeling and advertising of tobacco products
		Requires manufacturers and distributors of tobacco products to comply with regulations that establish product standards and that regulate the sale, distribution, promotion, and use of tobacco products
H.R. 1676	Prevent All Cigarette Trafficking Act of 2009	Preempts state, local, and tribal laws that require common carriers to verify the age of individuals who accept a tobacco delivery
H.R. 1676 (Continued)	Prevent All Cigarette Trafficking Act of 2009	Requires certain sellers to comply with certain requirements regarding reporting, shipping, recordkeeping, and collecting taxes
		Prohibits the mailing of tobacco products through the U.S. Postal Service
		Prohibits importers and interstate sellers of tobacco from selling cigarettes produced by companies that are not in full compliance with the terms of the tobacco settlement agreement between states and tobacco manufacturers and sellers
H.R. 2200	Transportation Security Administration Authorization Act	Requires airports to update security plans
		Preempts state and local laws governing background checks on individuals seeking to transport hazardous materials
H.R. 2221	Data Accountability and Trust Act	Preempts state laws that impose notification requirements in The event of a security breach
		Preempts state and local laws that require entities to implement security practices for handling personal information
H.R. 2647	National Defense authorization Act for Fiscal Year 2010	Preempts state laws relating to child custody proceedings
		Increases the costs of complying with existing intergovernmental mandates by increasing the number of service members and reservists eligible for protection under the Servicemembers Civil Relief Act
		Extends benefits for public employees under the Family and Medical Leave Act
H.R. 2652	Maritime Safety Act of 2009	Imposes safety and reporting requirements on public entities that operate vessels
		Preempts state and local laws that would be inconsistent with new standards
H.R. 2701	Intelligence Authorization Act for Fiscal Year 2010	Requires public entities, if subpoenaed, to provide evidence or Testimony
H.R. 2749	Food Safety Enhancement Act of 2009	Requires facilities that manufacture, process, pack, or hold food to register with the Secretary of Health and Human Services and pay an annual fee

Table 7. (Continued)

Bill Number (Committee or status)	Title of Legislation	Description of Mandate
		Requires entities that produce, manufacture, process, pack, transport, distribute, receive, hold, import, or export articles of food to comply with new safety standards and new procedures for recordkeeping and tracking
H.R. 2765	A bill to amend title 28, United States Code, to prohibit recognition and enforcement of foreign Defamation judgments and certain foreign judgments against the providers of interactive computer services	Preempts state laws related to foreign judgments
H.R. 2811	A bill to amend title 18, United States Code, to include constrictor snakes of the species Python genera as an injurious animal	Prohibits the importation and interstate transport of some snakes without a permit
H.R. 3126	Consumer Financial Protection Agency Act of 2009	Requires housing finance and student loan agencies to register with the Consumer Financial Protection Agency, provide whistleblower protection for their employees, meet standards for sales practices and examinations, comply with reporting requirements, and pay fees
		Requires public entities, if subpoenaed, to provide evidence or testimony
		Prohibits states from increasing the fees they levy on depository institutions for purposes of consumer compliance
		Requires state attorneys general to consult with the Office of the Comptroller of the Currency and the Consumer Financial Protection Agency before carrying out certain enforcement activities
		Preempts some state laws that protect consumers
H.R. 3371	Airline Safety and Pilot Training Improvement Act of 2009	Requires public entities that employ pilots to report to the Federal Aviation Administration and limit the amount of time their pilots can be on duty
H.R. 3570	Satellite Home Viewer Update	Requires copyright holders to participate in a process to set royalty rates for certain types of transmissions

Table 7. (Continued)

Bill Number (Committee or status)	Title of Legislation	Description of Mandate
	and Reauth-orization Act of 2009	Requires broadcasters and copyright holders to allow satellite providers to retransmit network signals of certain stations without paying royalties
		Increases the royalties that cable carriers pay for retransmitting the signals of distant network stations
		Requires cable carriers to pay filing fees to the Copyright Office for any royalty payments incurred from retransmitting distant network signals and allows copyright holders to audit their subscriber lists
		Limits the ability of copyright owners to collect comensation when secondary transmissions of copyrighted works are ade for emergency purposes
H.R. 3619	Coast Guard Authorization Act of 2010	Imposes safety and reporting requirements on public entities that operate vessels
		Increases the costs of complying with existing Intergover-nmental mandates by increasing the number of Coast Guard personnel eligible for protection under the Servicemembers Civil Relief Act
H.R. 3792	Ryan White HIV/AIDS Treatment Extension Act of 2009	Requires public medical facilities to comply with new procedures for notifying emergency response employees of possible exposures to an infectious disease
H.R. 3949	Veterans' Small Business Assistance and Servicemembe rs Protection Act of 2009	Prohibits residential utility providers, other service providers, and lessors of real property and motor vehicles from imposing early termination fees and other charges when service members cancel contracts
H.R. 3962	Affordable Health Care for America Act (Incorpor-ating the manager's amendment from November 3, 2009)	Requires public and private entities that handle health information to comply with new regulations
		Requires states to reimburse the federal government for any net increase in federal costs resulting from mandatory health insurance benefits established or maintained by the state
		Requires public and private owners and operators of vending machines to comply with standards for nutrition labeling
		Preempts state and local laws that establish periods for coverage under the Consolidated Omnibus Budget Reconciliation Act (COBRA) through a state high-risk pool if those laws would limit or prevent access to COBRA coverage because of the extension provided by the bill
		Preempts state laws that prevent the application of requirements and standards established in the bill for health Insurance coverage and employer-based health plans
		Preempts any state law preventing automatic payroll deductions of employee contributions to an employment-based health plan

Table 7. (Continued)

Bill Number (Committee or status)	Title of Legislation	Description of Mandate
		Preempts state and local laws that require the disclosure of the nutritional content of food offered for sale by restaurants, retail food establishments, and operators of vending machines if the laws' requirements are not similar to those specified in the bill
		Preempts state licensing laws in cases in which a health care professional is licensed in one state but provides services in another state under a contract or compact with a tribal health program
		Preempts state and local laws that require manufacturers of a drug, device, biological, or medical supply covered by the bill to disclose or report a payment or other transfer of value provided to a physician or teaching hospital
H.R. 3962	Affordable Health Care for	Requires public and private entities that handle health information to comply with new regulations
	America Act (Incorporating the manager's amendment from November 3, 2009, updated to reflect enactment of H.R. 3548)	Requires states to reimburse the federal government for any net increase in federal costs resulting from mandatory health insurance benefits established or maintained by the state
		Requires public and private owners and operators of vending machines to comply with standards for nutrition labeling
		Preempts state and local laws that establish periods for coverage under the Consolidated Omnibus Budget Reconciliation Act (COBRA) through a state high-risk pool if those laws would limit or prevent access to COBRA coverage because of the extension provided by the bill
		Preempts state laws that prevent the application of requirements and standards established in the bill for health Insurance coverage and employer-based health plans
		Preempts any state law preventing automatic payroll deductions of employee contributions to an employment-based health plan Preempts state and local laws that require the disclosure of the nutritional content of food offered for sale by restaurants, retail food establishments, and operators of vending machines if the laws' requirements are not similar to those specified in the bill
		Preempts state licensing laws in cases in which a health care professional is licensed in one state but provides services in another state under a contract or compact with a tribal health program
		Preempts state and local laws that require manufacturers of a drug, device, biological, or medical supply covered by the bill to disclose or report a payment or other transfer of value provided to a physician or teaching hospital
S. 38	Professional Boxing Amendments Act of 2009	Requires state and tribal boxing commissions to meet health and safety standards and to report information about boxing matches
		Requires public entities, if subpoenaed, to provide evidence or testimony

Table 7. (Continued)

Bill Number (Committee or status)	Title of Legislation	Description of Mandate
S. 69	Commission on Wartime Reloc-ation and Inter-nment of Latin Americans of Japanese Descent Act	Requires public entities, if subpoenaed, to provide evidence or testimony
S. 139	Data Breach Notification Act	Preempts state laws regarding notification in the event of a security breach
		Imposes notification requirements on state insurance Autho-rities and attorneys general
S. 313	White Mount-ain Apache Tri-be Water Rights Quantification Act of 2009	Requires the tribe to enact a water code
		Prohibits the tribe from objecting to the drilling or use of some wells
S. 375	Crow Tribe Water Rights Settlement	Requires the tribe to enact a water code
S. 475	Military Spo-uses Residency Relief Act	Prohibits states from collecting taxes on nonresident military spouses
S. 515	Patent Reform Act of 2009	Requires patent holders and applicants to pay fees
S. 599	Federal Firefi-ghters Fairness Act of 2009	Requires public medical facilities to comply with new procedures for notifying emergency response employees of possible exposures to an infectious disease
S. 728	Veterans' Ben-efits Enhance-ment Act of 2009	Requires state and local governments to grant wage and salary protection to service members
S. 982	Family Smok-ing Prevention and Tobacco Control Act	Preempts state laws governing tobacco products Requires tri-bal governments that manufacture or distribute tobacco prod-ucts to comply with new federal regulations and pay fees
S. 1194	Coast Guard Authorization Act for Fiscal Years 2010 and 2011	Increases the costs of complying with existing intergovernmental mandates by increasing the number of Coast Guard personnel eligible for protection under the Servicemembers Civil Relief Act
		Preempts state and local laws governing access to the Atlantic Intercoastal Waterway
		Preempts state and local laws governing vessels that transfer oil
S. 1261	Providing for Additional Sec-urity in States'	Requires states to have security and privacy policies for personally identifiable information and to have a process for individuals to amend their data

Table 7. (Continued)

Bill Number (Committee or status)	Title of Legislation	Description of Mandate
	Identification Act of 2009	
S. 1390	National Defense Authorization Act for Fiscal Year 2010	Increases the costs of complying with existing intergovernmental mandates by increasing the number of service members and reservists eligible for protection under the Servicemembers Civil Relief Act
S. 1451	FAA Air Transportation Modernization and Safety Improvement Act	Requires public entities that own aircraft or helicopters to install equipment and adhere to safety procedures
		Requires airports to submit contingency plans for emergency circumstances
		Requires states to allow the Federal Aviation Administration access to criminal history records
S. 1462	American Clean Energy Leadership Act of 2009	Requires electric utilities to certify that a minimum percentage of their sales came from renewable sources
		Requires electric utilities to connect small generation facilities to their power system and to develop plans for regional transmission projects
		Imposes a mandate if the Federal Energy Regulatory Commission (FERC) uses eminent domain to acquire rights-of- way for new transmission projects
		Requires owners and operators of electric infrastructure to comply with cybersecurity rules
		Requires states to certify to the Department of Energy that they have (or have not) updated their residential and commercial building codes to meet new standards
		Requires public entities to report to the Energy Information Administration
		Preempts state law by authorizing FERC to issue construction permits for transmission projects when a state has rejected a request for a permit
		Preempts state laws relating to the energy efficiency of various products
S. 1490	Personal Data Privacy and Security Act of 2009	Preempts state laws regarding the treatment of personal information
		Imposes notification requirements on state attorneys general and insurance authorities
S. 1494	Intelligence Authorization Act for Fiscal Year 2010	Requires public entities, if subpoenaed, to provide evidence or testimony
S. 1670	Satellite Television Modernization Act of 2009	Requires copyright holders to participate in a process to set royalty rates for certain types of transmissions
		Requires broadcasters and copyright holders to allow satellite providers to retransmit network signals of certain stations without paying royalties

Table 7. (Continued)

Bill Number (Committee or status)	Title of Legislation	Description of Mandate
		Requires low-power stations to allow satellite carriers to provide secondary transmissions to subscribers within a local market without paying royalties
		Increases the royalties that cable carriers pay for retransmitting the signals of distant network stations

Source: Congressional Budget Office.

a. In certain cases, proposed legislation reviewed by CBO contained multiple mandates, some of which did not have costs exceeding the statutory threshold.

Table 8. Bills Reviewed by CBO in 2009 That Contain Private-Sector Mandates.

Of the 419 bills or legislative proposals that the Congressional Budget Office reviewed in 2009 for mandates as defined in the Unfunded Mandates Reform Act, 105 contained private-sector mandates. Of those 105 bills, 27 contained mandates with aggregate costs that CBO estimated would exceed the statutory threshold in UMRA ($139 million in 2009). Some bills were considered by more than one committee; in those cases, the table lists the various versions of that bill.
Bills containing private-sector mandates whose aggregate costs are estimated to exceed the threshold are listed first in the table. Mandates with costs above the statutory threshold are shown in bold type, mandates with uncertain costs are in italic type, and mandates with costs below the threshold are in regular type.

Bill Number (Committee or status)	Title of Legislation	Description of Mandate
Bills Containing Private-Sector Mandates with Aggregate Costs Above the Statutory Threshold[a]		
H.R. 1	American Recovery and Reinvestment Act of 2009	**Modifies the requirements and conditions of continued coverage under the Consolidated Omnibus Budget Reconciliation Act (COBRA) for certain employers who offer group health insurance**
		Modifies regulations related to limitations on the use of certain business losses in unprofitable years following a change in ownership[b]
		Requires entities to comply with new regulations related to the use, disclosure, and privacy of health information
H.R. 1	American Recovery and Reinvestment Act of 2009 (Amendment in the	**Modifies the requirements and conditions of continued coverage under the Consolidated Omnibus Budget Reconciliation Act (COBRA) for certain employers who offer group health insurance**

Table 8. (Continued)

Bill Number (Committee or status)	Title of Legislation	Description of Mandate
	nature of a substitute, as introduced by Senators Inouye and Baucus on January 31, 2009)	**Modifies regulations related to limitations on the use of certain business losses in unprofitable years following a change in ownership**[b]
		Requires private entities to comply with new regulations related to the use, disclosure, and privacy of health information
H.R. 627	Credit Cardholders' Bill of Rights Act of 2009	**Prevents creditors from completing any transaction in excess of a credit limit and charging over-the-limit fees**
		Requires creditors to report additional data about credit card transactions, fees, and rates
		Prohibits individuals from paying fees with credit made available by a credit card with certain fees in the first year
		Prohibits creditors from issuing credit cards to individuals under the age of 18, charging fees for certain payments, and using the term "prime rate" in some instances
		Requires creditors to provide information to consumers on activations, interest rates, and payoff balances
H.R. 786	A bill to make permanent the tempor-ary increase in deposit insurance coverage, and for other purposes	**Requires depository institutions to pay higher premiums by making permanent the increase in deposit insurance coverage**
		Requires bank holding companies to pay special assessments
H.R. 915	FAA Reauthorization Act of 2009	**Prohibits the operation of certain aircraft that are not in compliance with low-noise standards**
		Ends antitrust immunity for international air carrier alliances, requiring affected air carriers to reapply under new standards
		Requires airports to meet new firefighting standards
		Requires entities registered with the Federal Aviation Administration to comply with a new schedule of fees for certain services and activities
		Imposes several new requirements on air carriers related to airline employees and passenger service
H.R. 1106	Helping Families Save Their Homes Act	**Requires depository institutions to pay higher premiums by making permanent the increase in deposit insurance coverage**
		Allows bankruptcy judges to modify the rights of claimholders by making changes to the terms of home mortgage agreements
		Prevents investors from seeking damages for contract violations under some circumstances

Table 8. (Continued)

Bill Number (Committee or status)	Title of Legislation	Description of Mandate
		Requires bank holding companies to pay special assessments
		Prevents investors in residential mortgages from suing servicers of those loans under some circumstances
		Requires mortgage claimholders to file timely notice with the court before adding fees, costs, or charges while a bankruptcy case is pending
H.R. 1256 (Energy and Commerce)	Family Smoking Prevention and Tobacco Control Act	**Imposes a fee on manufacturers and importers of tobacco products to cover the cost to the Food and Drug Administration of regulating those products**
		Imposes new requirements related to the labeling and advertising of tobacco products
		Requires manufacturers and distributors of tobacco products to comply with regulations that establish product standards and regulate the sale, distribution, promotion, and use of tobacco products
H.R. 1256 (Oversight and Government Reform)	Family Smoking Prevention and Tobacco Control Act	**Imposes a fee on manufacturers and importers of tobacco products to cover the cost to the Food and Drug Administration of regulating those products**
		Imposes new requirements related to the labeling and advertising of tobacco products
		Requires manufacturers and distributors of tobacco products to comply with regulations that establish product standards and regulate the sale, distribution, promotion, and use of tobacco products
H.R. 1256 (As passed by the House)	Family Smoking Prevention and Tobacco Control Act	**Imposes a fee on manufacturers and importers of tobacco products to cover the cost to the Food and Drug Administration of regulating those products**
		Imposes new requirements related to the labeling and advertising of tobacco products
		Requires manufacturers and distributors of tobacco products to comply with regulations that establish product standards and regulate the sale, distribution, promotion, and use of tobacco products
H.R. 2221	Data Accountability and Trust Act	**Requires information brokers to establish accuracy standards for personal information and to maintain an audit log of access to or transmission of any data containing personal information**
		Requires certain entities that own or possess personal information, are engaged in interstate commerce, or have a contract with a third party to maintain such data, to establish and implement information security policies and procedures

Table 8. (Continued)

Bill Number (Committee or status)	Title of Legislation	Description of Mandate
		Requires entities that own or possess data in elect-ronic form containing personal information, and other third parties, to provide notification follow-ing a security breach
		Requires information brokers to submit their policies for information security to the Federal Trade Commission for review
H.R. 2410	Foreign Relations Auth-orization Act, Fiscal Years 2010 and 2011	**Makes permanent the authority of the Secretary of State to collect a surcharge on passport applications**
H.R. 2454	American Clean Energy and Security Act of 2009	**Requires covered facilities to participate in a cap-and-trade program to reduce greenhouse gas emissions**
		Requires producers and importers of hydrofluoricarbons (HFCs) to participate in a cap-and-trade program and imposes other restrictions on the use of HFCs
		Requires electric utilities to pay assessments based on the amount of electricity delivered to retail customers
		Establishes efficiency standards for lighting and appliances
		Establishes performance standards for new coal-fueled power plants and facilities not covered by the cap-and-trade program and authorizes standards for reducing black carbon emissions
		Imposes position limits, transaction fees, and reporting requirements on participants in certain commodities markets
		Establishes emission standards for vehicles and vehicle engines and authorizes a standard for the manufacture of certain vehicles
		Authorizes an international reserve allowance program for importers of carbon-intensive goods
		Requires electric utilities to certify that a minimum percentage of their sales comes from renewable sources
		Creates and expands reporting and planning requirements for entities that produce greenhouse gas emissions
H.R. 2749	Food Safety Enhancement Act of 2009	**Requires facilities that manufacture, process, pack, or hold food to register with the Secretary of Health and Human Services and pay an annual fee**
		Requires entities that produce, manufacture, process, pack, transport, distribute, receive, hold,

Table 8. (Continued)

Bill Number (Committee or status)	Title of Legislation	Description of Mandate
		import, or export articles of food to comply with safety standards and new procedures for Record-keeping and tracking
H.R. 2998	American Clean Energy and Security Act	**Requires covered facilities to participate in a cap-and-trade program to reduce greenhouse gas emissions**
		Requires producers and importers of hydrofluoric-arbons (HFCs) to participate in a cap-and-trade program and imposes other restrictions on the use of HFCs
		Requires electric utilities to pay assessments based on the amount of electricity delivered to retail customers
		Establishes efficiency standards for lighting and Appliances
		Establishes performance standards for new coal-fueled power plants and facilities not covered by the cap-and-trade program and authorizes
		standards for reducing black carbon emissions
		Imposes position limits, transaction fees, and reporting requirements on participants in certain commodities markets
		Establishes emission standards for vehicles and vehicle engines and authorizes a standard for the manufacture of certain vehicles
		Authorizes an international reserve allowance program for importers of carbon-intensive goods
		Imposes a mandate if the Federal Energy Regulatory Commission uses eminent domain to acquire rights-of-way for new transmission projects
		Requires electric utilities to certify that a minimum percentage of their sales comes from renewable sources
		Creates and expands reporting and planning requirements for entities that produce greenhouse gas emissions
		Requires private entities, if subpoenaed, to provide evidence or Testimony
H.R. 3126	Consumer Financial Protection Agency Act of 2009	**Requires nondepository entities to pay fees to the Consumer Finance Protection Agency (CFPA)**
		Requires financial companies to register with the CFPA, provide whistle-blower protection for their employees, meet standards for sales practices and examinations, and comply with reporting Requi-rements

Table 8. (Continued)

Bill Number (Committee or status)	Title of Legislation	Description of Mandate
		Requires private entities, if subpoenaed, to provide evidence or testimony
H.R. 3590	Patient Protection and Affordable Care Act (Amendment in the nature of a substitute proposed in the Senate on November 18, 2009)	**Requires individuals to obtain acceptable coverage**
		Assesses a fee on medium-sized and large employ-yers that did not offer health insurance to their em-ployees if any of their workers obtained subsidized coverage through the insurance exchanges
		Prohibits health insurers from establishing lifetime limits and unreasonable annual limits; from resc-inding coverage except in certain cases such as fraud; from imposing any exclusions of coverage for preexisting conditions; from varying premium rates on the basis of factors other than those spec-ified in the bill; and, with regard to coverage, from discriminating against individuals on the basis of health status or salary
		Requires health insurers to accept every employer or individual in the state for coverage, guarantee renewability of coverage, offer coverage of certain preventive health services without cost sharing, and extend dependent coverage until the age of 26
		Requires health insurers to accept every employer or individual in the state for coverage, guarantee renewability of coverage, offer coverage of certain preventive health services without cost sharing, and extend dependent coverage until the age of 26
		Requires public and private hospitals operating in the United States to establish, update, and make public a list of standard charges for the items and services they Provide
		Requires restaurants and retail food establishments that are part of a chain with 20 or more locations and owners or operators of vending machines to comply with standards for nutrition labeling
		Assesses an excise tax on policyholders whose premiums exceed a specified amount[b]
		Requires public and private entities that handle health information to comply with new regulations
H.R. 3590	Patient Protection and Affordable Care Act (Amendment in the nature of a substitute, incorporating the	**Requires individuals to obtain acceptable coverage**
		Assesses a fee on medium-sized and large employers that did not offer health insurance to their employees if any of their workers obtained

Table 8. (Continued)

Bill Number (Committee or status)	Title of Legislation	Description of Mandate
	manager's amendment released on December 19, 2009)	**subsidized coverage through the insurance exchanges**
		Prohibits health insurers from establishing lifetime limits and unreasonable annual limits; from rescinding coverage except in certain cases such as fraud; from imposing any exclusions of coverage for preexisting conditions; from varying premium rates on the basis of factors other than those specified in the bill; and, with regard to coverage, from discriminating against individuals on the basis of health status or salary
		Requires health insurers to accept every employer or individual in the state for coverage, guarantee renewability of coverage, offer coverage of certain preventive health services without cost sharing, and extend dependent coverage until the age of 26
		Requires public and private hospitals operating in the United States to establish, update, and make public a list of standard charges for the items and services they provide
		Requires restaurants and retail food establishments that are part of a chain with 20 or more locations and owners or operators of vending machines to comply with standards for nutrition labeling
		Assesses an excise tax on policyholders whose premiums exceed a specified amount[b]
		Requires public and private entities that handle health information to comply with new regulations
H.R. 3639	Expedited CARD Reform for Consumers Act of 2009	**Accelerates the implementation of several requirements on creditors**
H.R. 3962	Affordable Health Care for America Act (Incorporating the manager's amendment from November 3, 2009)	**Requires individuals to obtain acceptable health insurance coverage**
		Requires employers to either offer health insurance to their employees or pay an excise tax to the federal government
		Prohibits health insurers from establishing lifetime limits, rescinding coverage except in cases of fraud, treating acts of domestic violence as preexisting conditions, and reducing retiree health benefits after a participant retires
		Requires health insurers to extend coverage of dependents until the age of 26, reduce the period that enrollees can be excluded from coverage because of preexisting conditions, submit justification for increases in premiums, provide

Table 8. (Continued)

Bill Number (Committee or status)	Title of Legislation	Description of Mandate
		coverage for treatment of a child's congenital or developmental deformities, and provide rebates to enrollees if medical loss ratios (the fraction of health insurance premiums spent on health care services) fall below a level specified by the Secretary of Health and Human Services
		Places limits on certain agreements between drug manufacturers for settling patent infringement claims
		Requires restaurants and retail food establishments that are part of a chain with 20 or more locations and owners or operators of vending machines to comply With standards for nutrition labeling
		Imposes an income tax surcharge on high-income individuals[b]
		Requires employers to extend the period of eligibi-lity for health insurance coverage under the Cons-olidated Omnibus Budget Reconciliation Act (COBRA)
		Permits the Secretary of Health and Human servi-ces to impose sanctions on health insurers who en-courage enrollees who may qualify for participate-on in the national high-risk pool program to cancel their coverage
		Requires public and private entities that handle
		health information to comply with new regulations
H.R. 3962	Affordable Health Care for America Act (Incor-porating the manager's amendment from Nove-mber 3, 2009, updated to reflect enactment of H.R. 3548)	**Requires individuals to obtain acceptable health insurance coverage**
		Requires employers to either offer health insurance to their employees or pay an excise tax to the federal government
		Prohibits health insurers from establishing lifetime limits, rescinding coverage except in cases of fraud, treating acts of domestic violence as preexisting conditions, and reducing retiree health benefits after a participant retires
		Requires health insurers to extend coverage of dependents until the age of 26, reduce the period that enrollees can be excluded from coverage because of preexisting conditions, submit justification for increases in premiums, provide coverage for treatment of a child's congenital or enrollees if medical loss ratios (the fraction of health insurance premiums spent on health care services) fall below a level specified by the Secretary of Health and Human Services

Table 8. (Continued)

Bill Number (Committee or status)	Title of Legislation	Description of Mandate
		Places limits on certain agreements between drug manufacturers for settling patent infringement claims
		Requires restaurants and retail food establishments thatare part of a chain with 20 or more locations and owners or operators of vending machines to comply with standards for nutrition labeling
		Imposes an income tax surcharge on high-income individuals[b]
		Requires employers to extend the period of eligibility forhealth insurance coverage under the Consolidated Omnibus Budget Reconciliation Act (COBRA)
		Permits the Secretary of Health and Human Services to impose sanctions on health insurers who encourage enrollees who may qualify for participation in the national high-risk pool program to cancel their coverage
		Requires public and private entities that handle health Information to comply with new regulations
H.R. 4173 (Introduced)	Wall Street Reform and Consumer Protection Act of 2009	**Requires large financial institutions to pay fees** **Requires nondepository entities to pay fees**
		Creates a fiduciary duty for broker dealers that provide investment advice
		Imposes requirements for prudential standards, reporting, and planning on entities that engage in financial activities
		Imposes position limits, transaction fees, and reporting requirements on participants in swaps
		Requires financial companies to register with the Consumer Financial Protection Agency, provide whistle-blower protection for their employees, meet standards for sales practices and Examin-ations, and comply with reporting requirements
		Establishes new requirements for compensation at publicly traded companies
		Prohibits certain compensation agreements by financial institutions with assets of at least $1 billion and requires such institutions to disclose information about compensation
		Requires national securities exchanges and associa-tions to prohibit the listing of any security by a com-pany in violation of certain compensation standards
		Requires institutional investment managers to disclose the results of shareholders' votes on compensation

Table 8. (Continued)

Bill Number (Committee or status)	**Title of Legislation**	**Description of Mandate**
		Requires organizations that provide clearing services for derivatives to designate a compliance officer, monitor trading to prevent price manipulation, and comply with standards for collecting and maintaining data
		Requires hedge funds and private equity firms to register with the Securities and Exchange Commission (SEC) and requires private fund advisers to submit information to the SEC upon Request
		Requires nationally recognized statistical rating organizations to comply with several requirements with respect to disclosures, reports, certain policies, employees, and services provided that are unrelated to credit-rating services
H.R. 4173 (Rules)	Wall Street Reform and Consumer Protection Act of 2009	**Requires large financial institutions to pay fees** **Requires nondepository entities to pay fees**
		Creates a fiduciary duty for broker dealers that provide investment advice
		Imposes requirements for prudential standards, reporting, and planning on entities that engage in financial activities
		Imposes position limits, transaction fees, and reporting requirements on participants in swaps
		Requires financial companies to register with the Consumer Financial Protection Agency, provide whistle-blower protection for their employees,
		meet standards for sales practices and Examinations, and comply with reporting requirements
H.R. 4173 (Rules) (Continued)	Wall Street Reform and Consumer Protection Act of 2009	*Establishes new requirements for compensation at publicly traded companies*
		Prohibits certain compensation agreements by financial institutions with assets of at least $1 billion and requires such institutions to disclose information about compensation
		Requires securitizers to ensure that mortgage debtors are able to make their mortgage payments
		Prohibits creditors from charging some fees and from issuing some types of mortgages
		Prohibits mortgage servicers, under some circumstances, from obtaining hazard insurance on behalf of debtors and charging them for the costs of the insurance and other fees
		Requires national securities exchanges and associations to prohibit the listing of any security by a company in violation of certain compensation standards

Table 8. (Continued)

Bill Number (Committee or status)	Title of Legislation	Description of Mandate
		Requires institutional investment managers to disclose the results of shareholders' votes on compensation
		Requires organizations that provide clearing services for derivatives to designate a compliance officer, monitor trading to prevent price manipulation, and comply with standards for collecting and maintaining data
		Requires hedge funds and private equity firms to register with the Securities and Exchange Commi-ssion (SEC) and requires private fund advisers to submit information to the SEC upon request
		Requires nationally recognized statistical rating organizations to comply with several requirements with respect to disclosures, reports, certain policies, employees, and services provided that are unrelated to credit-rating services
S. 414	Credit Card Accoun-tability Responsibility and Disclosure Act of 2009	**Places limits on fees and interest charges that creditors could collect**
		Prohibits issuers of gift cards from collecting certain fees and establishing expiration dates
		Requires creditors to report additional data about credit card operations, fees, and other information
		Prohibits the issuance of credit cards to people under the age of 21 unless certain requirements are met Imposes several requirements on creditors regarding account payment methods, terms, and disclosures
		Imposes a fee on manufacturers and importers of tobacco products to cover the cost to the Food and Drug Administration of regulating those products
		Imposes new requirements related to the labeling and advertising of tobacco products
		Requires manufacturers and distributors of tobacco products to comply with regulations that establish product standards and regulate the sale, distribu-tion, promotion, and use of tobacco products
S. 1451	FAA Air Transportation Modernization and Safety Improvement Act	**Prohibits the operation of certain aircraft that are not in compliance with low-noise standards**
		Requires owners of aircraft to install two different types of next-generation equipment on their aircraft
		Requires operators of helicopters and fixed-wing aircraft for emergency medical service to install equipment and adhere to safety procedures

Table 8. (Continued)

Bill Number (Committee or status)	Title of Legislation	Description of Mandate
		Requires airports to submit reports and continge-ncy plans for emergency circumstances
		Imposes several new requirements on air carriers related to airline employees and passenger service
S. 1490	Personal Data Privacy and Security Act of 2009	**Requires businesses to enhance their security standards to include the ability to trace access to and transmission of all records containing personally identifiable information and to establish other programs for data privacy and security**
		Requires data brokers to comply with new requirements for disclosure and data collection
		Requires any entity taking an adverse action with respect to an individual on the basis of information contained in a personal electronic record to notify the individual
		Requires entities that own or possess data in electronic form containing personal information, and other third parties, to provide notification following a security breach
S. 1733	Clean Energy Jobs and American Power Act	**Requires covered facilities to participate in a cap-and-trade program to reduce greenhouse gas emissions**
		Requires producers and importers of hydrofluorocarbons (HFCs) to participate in a cap-and-trade program and imposes other restrictions on the use of HFCs
		Requires electric utilities to pay assessments based on the amount of electricity delivered to retail customers
		Establishes standards for new coal-fueled power
		plants and geological storage of carbon dioxide and authorizes standards for reducing black carbon emissions
		Establishes standards for greenhouse gas emissions from certain vehicles and engines
		Requires private entities to comply with new energy-efficiency standards in state and local building codes
		Creates and expands reporting requirements for entities that produce greenhouse gas emissions
Bills Containing Private-Sector Mandates Whose Aggregate Costs Could Not Be Determined		
H.R. 200	Helping Families Save Their Homes in Bankruptcy Act of 2009	*Allows bankruptcy judges to modify the rights of claimholders by making changes to the terms of home mortgage agreements*

Table 8. (Continued)

Bill Number (Committee or status)	Title of Legislation	Description of Mandate
		Requires mortgage claimholders to file timely notice with the court before adding fees, costs, or charges while a bankruptcy case is pending
H.R. 233	Railroad Antitrust Enforcement Act of 2009	*Subjects railroad carriers to certain antitrust statutes*
H.R. 515	Radioactive Import Deterrence Act	*Prohibits the importation of low-level radioactive waste*
H.R. 848	Performance Rights Act	*Requires over-the-air radio broadcasters to pay new royalty fees to holders of copyrights on sound recordings*
H.R. 977	Derivatives Markets Transparency and Accountability Act of 2009	*Imposes position limits, transaction fees, and reporting requirements on participants in certain commodities markets*
		Authorizes the Commodity Futures Trading Commission to suspend trading in credit default swaps under some circumstances
		Imposes new requirements on exchanges and organizations that provide clearing services for derivatives
H.R. 1575	End Government Reimbursement of Excessive Executive Disbursements (End GREED) Act	*Imposes a mandate if individuals are required to pay back certain compensation received from companies*
H.R. 1664	A bill to amend the executive compensation provisions of the Emergency Economic Stabilization Act of 2008 to prohibit unreasonable and excessive compensation and compensation not based on performance standards	*Imposes a mandate if existing compensation arrangements between some financial institutions that have received federal funds and executives or employees of those institutions are invalidated*
H.R. 1728	Mortgage Reform and Anti-Predatory Lending Act	*Establishes requirements for creditors, loan originators, mortgage servicers, real estate appraisers, and other entities that participate in the mortgage industry*
		Requires entities that acquire foreclosed properties to honor tenants' leases
		Requires securitizers to ensure that mortgage debtors are able to make their mortgage payments
H.R. 2194	Iran Refined Petroleum Sanctions Act of 2009	*Extends and expands sanctions under the Iran Sanctions Act, which could impose requirements on entities engaged in transactions with businesses or countries subject to sanctions under the act*

Table 8. (Continued)

Bill Number (Committee or status)	Title of Legislation	Description of Mandate
H.R. 2647	National Defense Authorization Act for Fiscal Year 2010	*Increases the costs of complying with existing private-sector mandates by increasing the number of service members and reservists eligible for protection under the Servicemembers Civil Relief Act*
		Extends the employment benefits of the Family and Medical Leave Act to certain service members and veterans
H.R. 2652	Maritime Safety Act of 2009	*Establishes new safety requirements for commercial and recreational vessels*
		Requires businesses in the maritime industry to comply with recordkeeping requirements and provide protection for whistle-blowers
H.R. 2868 (Energy and Commerce)	Chemical Facility Anti-Terrorism Act of 2009	*Expands and makes permanent existing security requirements on owners and operators of certain chemical facilities*
		Requires high-risk facilities with chemicals to conduct assessments of plans and procedures to reduce the incidence of terrorism
		Provides whistle-blower protection to employees of chemical facilities
H.R. 2868 (Homeland Security)	Chemical Facility Anti-Terrorism Act of 2009	*Expands and makes permanent existing security requirements on owners and operators of certain chemical facilities*
		Requires high-risk facilities with chemicals to conduct assessments of plans and procedures to reduce the incidence of terrorism
		Provides whistle-blower protection to employees of chemical facilities
H.R. 2989	401(k) Fair Disclosure and Pension Security Act of 2009	*Requires service providers of defined-contribution retirement plans subject to the Employee etirement Income Security Act of 1974 (ERISA) to supply a written statement to the administrator of the plan*
		Requires certain plan administrators to provide participants with additional information about their investment options
		Prohibits providers of investment services to defined-contribution plans subject to ERISA from supplying investment advice to those plans and imposes requirements on other service providers that supply investment advice to plans
		Requires contributing plan sponsors of defined-benefit retirement plans subject to ERISA to comply with recordkeeping requirements
		Extends the time period for single-employer defined-benefit plans to amortize adjusted funding shortfalls measured in 2009 and 2010[b,c]

Table 8. (Continued)

Bill Number (Committee or status)	Title of Legislation	Description of Mandate
H.R. 3269	Corporate and Financial Institution Compensation Fairness Act of 2009	*Establishes new requirements for compensation at publicly traded companies*
		Prohibits certain compensation agreements by financial institutions with assets of at least $1 billion and requires such institutions to disclose information about compensation
		Requires national securities exchanges and associa-tions to prohibit the listing of any security by a com-pany in violation of certain compensation standards
		Requires institutional investment managers to disclose the results of shareholders' votes on compensation
H.R. 3371 H.R. 3619	Airline Safety and Pilot Training Improvement Act of 2009	*Requires air carriers to hire pilots who have a certain level of experience and to develop safety programs for pilots, including training and a mentoring program*
		Requires air carriers to evaluate information about pilots, submit flight histories for pilots, and possibly limit the number of hours the pilots it employs can be on duty
		Requires sellers of tickets for air carriers to provide information for each leg of the flight before the sale
	Coast Guard Authorization Act of 2010	*Establishes new safety requirements for commercial and recreational vessels*
		Requires businesses in the maritime industry to co-mply with requirements for security and recordke-eping and to provide protection for whistle-blowers
		Increases the costs of complying with existing private-sector mandates by raising the number of Coast Guard personnel eligible for protection
		under the Servicemembers Civil Relief Act
		Requires owners and operators of cruise lines to meet certain safety standards
H.R. 3795 (Agriculture)	Derivative Markets Transparency and Accountability Act of 2009	*Imposes position limits, transaction fees, and reporting requirements on participants in swaps*
		Requires organizations that provide clearing services for derivatives to designate a compliance officer, monitor trading to prevent price manip-ulation, and comply with standards for collecting and maintaining data
H.R. 3795 (Financial Services)	Over-the-Counter Derivatives Markets Act of 2009	*Imposes position limits, transaction fees, and reporting requirements on participants in swaps*
		Requires organizations that provide clearing services for derivatives to designate a compliance officer, monitor trading to prevent price manip-ulation, and comply with standards for collecting and maintaining data

Table 8. (Continued)

Bill Number (Committee or status)	Title of Legislation	Description of Mandate
S. 146 S. 685	Railroad Antitrust Enforcement Act of 2009 Oil Spill Prevention Act of 2009	*Subjects railroad carriers to certain antitrust statutes Requires merchant mariners to comply with new medical standards established by the U.S. Coast Guard*
		Requires shipowners to pay certain expenses of seamen who are abandoned under certain conditions
S. 787	Clean Water Restoration Act	*Requires private entities to obtain permits for activities that would affect certain bodies of water*
S. 962	Enhanced Partnership with Pakistan Act of 2009	*Prohibits the export of defense equipment to Paki-stan in the absence of certification and a waiver by the Secretary of State*
S. 1194	Coast Guard Authorization Act for Fiscal Years 2010 and 2011	*Requires certain facilities and vessels to meet new safety standards when transferring oil*
		Requires certain vessels to establish and maintain evidence of financial responsibility sufficient to meet their liability in the event of an oil spill
		Imposes a mandate on towing vessels if safety requirements are accelerated
		Increases the costs of complying with existing private-sector mandates by increasing the number of Coast Guard personnel eligible for protection under the Servicemembers Civil Relief Act
S. 1390	National Defense Authorization Act for Fiscal Year 2010	*Increases the costs of complying with existing private-sector mandates by increasing the number of service members and reservists eligible for pro-tection under the Servicemembers Civil Relief Act*
S. 1462	American Clean Energy Leadership Act of 2009	*Requires owners and operators of electric infrastructure to comply with cybersecurity rules*
		Imposes a mandate if the Federal Energy
		Regulatory Commission uses eminent domain to acquire rights-of-way for new transmission projects
		Establishes new energy conservation standards for commercial furnaces and lighting products
		Requires electric utilities to certify that a minimum percentage of their sales came from renewable sources
		Requires electric utilities to connect small generation facilities to their power system and develop plans for regional transmission projects
		Requires private entities to report to the Energy Information Administration
S. 2799	Comprehensive Iran Sanctions, Account-ability,and Divestment Act of 2009	*Bans all imports from and some exports to Iran*
		Extends and expands sanctions under the Iran Sanctions Act, which could impose mandates on entities engaged in transactions with businesses or countries subject to sanctions under the act

Table 8. (Continued)

Bill Number (Committee or status)	Title of Legislation	Description of Mandate
		Freezes the assets of family members and certain associates of Iranian government officials subject to sanctions Imposes new license requirements on exporters of certain products
H.R. 2	Children's Health Insurance Program Reauthorization Act of 2009	Requires group health plans to permit employees to enroll in the group health plan if they lose eligibility for Medicaid or the Children's Health Insurance Program or become eligible through those programs for assistance in paying premiums
		Requires employers to inform employees of potential opportunities for assistance in paying premiums
H.R. 42	Commission on Wartime Relocation and Intern-ment of Latin Americans of Japanese Descent Act	Requires private entities, if subpoenaed, to provide evidence or testimony
H.R. 80	Captive Primate Safety Act	Prohibits the sale or transport of nonhuman prima-tes in interstate and foreign commerce without a license or permit
H.R. 384	TARP [Troubled Assets Relief Program] Reform and Accountability Act	Prohibits investors in residential mortgages from suing servicers of those loans under some circumstances
		Imposes a mandate if entities are prohibited from seeking damages under certain antitrust laws for negotiations authorized under the bill
H.R. 466	Wounded Veteran Job Security Act	Requires employers to retain veterans who miss work because of medical treatment for a servicecon-nected injury and to grant seniority and other bene-fits to those veterans as if they had not been absent
H.R. 512	Federal Election Integrity Act of 2009	Prohibits the chief election administration official of a state from taking an active part in political management or in a political campaign with resp-ect to any federal election over which the official has supervisory authority
H.R. 788	A bill to provide a safe harbor for mortgage Ser-vicers who engage in spe-cified mortgage loan mo-dification, and for other purposes	Prohibits investors in residential mortgages from suing servicers of those loans under some circumstances
		Imposes reporting requirements on mortgage servicers
H.R. 860	Coral Reef Conservation Act Reauthorization and Enhancement Amend-ments of 2009	Makes private entities liable for damages to coral reefs within the jurisdiction of the United States
		Requires private entities to obtain permits for activities that could affect coral reefs
H.R. 911	Stop Child Abuse in Residential Programs for Teens Act of 2009	Imposes training and disclosure requirements and establishes minimum health and safety requirem-ents on operators of residential programs that treat

Table 8. (Continued)

Bill Number (Committee or status)	Title of Legislation	Description of Mandate
		youth who have emotional, behavioral, mental health, or substance abuse problems
H.R. 1084	Commercial Advertise-ment Loudness Mitigat-ion (CALM) Act	Imposes limits on sound volume for broadcasters and video, satellite, and cable providers
H.R. 1147	Local Community Radio Act of 2009	Imposes a mandate if licenses authorizing low-power FM stations to broadcast on second-adjacent channels were to be invalidated
H.R. 1253	Health Insurance Restr-ictions and Limitations Clarification Act of 2009	Requires group health plans to disclose the limitations and restrictions on health insurance coverage in a timely manner to the plans' sponsors and participants
H.R. 1259	Dextromethorphan Distribution Act of 2009	Restricts the distribution, possession, and receipt of unfinished dextromethorphan to entities authorized under federal or state laws
		Requires a seller of unfinished dextromethorphan to confirm that the buyer is legally allowed to make the purchase
H.R. 1262	Water Quality Investment Act of 2009	Increases tonnage duties on certain vessels entering ports in the United States
H.R. 1319	Informed P2P [Peer-to-Peer] User Act	Requires companies that develop or distribute software that allows files to be shared between computers to provide certain features that give the user control over various functions of the software
H.R. 1676	Prevent All Cigarette Trafficking Act of 2009	Requires certain sellers to comply with certain requirements regarding reporting, shipping, recordkeepin, and collecting taxes
		Requires common carriers to comply with recordkeeping requirements
		Prohibits the mailing of tobacco products through the U.S. Postal Service
		Prohibits importers and interstate sellers of tobacco from selling cigarettes produced by companies that are not in full compliance with the terms of the tobacco settlement agreement between states and tobacco manufacturers and sellers
H.R. 1916	Migratory Bird Habitat Investment and Enhancement Act	Increases the annual fee for the Duck Stamp that serves as a federal license required for hunting migratory waterfowl
H.R. 2190	Mercury Pollution Reduction Act	Prohibits the export and use of mercury by facilities that manufacture chlorine or caustic soda
H.R. 2200	Transportation Security Administration Authorization Act	Requires airports to update security plans
		Requires all members of the cabin crew of U.S. air carriers to take five hours of training in advanced self-defense methods biannually

Table 8. (Continued)

Bill Number (Committee or status)	Title of Legislation	Description of Mandate
		Requires operators of motor vehicles to obtain a valid biometric transportation security card in order to transport securitysensitive materials
H.R. 2701	Intelligence Authorization Act for Fiscal Year 2010	Extends the requirement for private entities, if subpoenaed, to provide evidence or testimony
H.R. 2765	A bill to amend title 28, United States Code, to prohibit recognition and enforcement of foreign defamation judgments and certain foreign judgments against the providers of interactive computer services	Prohibits a U.S. court from enforcing a foreign defamation judgment in certain cases, limiting an existing right to recover damages
H.R. 2811	A bill to amend title 18, United States Code, to Include constrictor snakes of the species Python genera as an injurious animal	Prohibits the importation and interstate transport of certain snakes without a permit
H.R. 2994	Satellite Home Viewer Reauthorization Act of 2009	Extends an authorization for satellite providers to retransmit distant signals to unserved households without obtaining consent or providing compensateion to broadcasters
		Extends an existing mandate that prohibits broadcasters from entering into certain exclusive contracts for the rights to retransmit their programs
		Requires satellite carriers that provide local high-definition (HD) channels to also provide HD
		signals for local noncommercial, educational stations
H.R. 3258	Drinking Water System Security Act of 2009	Imposes new security requirements on drinking water facilities
H.R. 3342	Aamodt Litigation Settlement Act	Imposes a mandate if the Secretary of the Interior condemns property to implement the settlement
H.R. 3360	Cruise Vessel Security and Safety Act of 2009	Requires certain cruise vessels to meet safety standards, comply with disclosure and recordkeeping requirements, limit the access of crew members to passengers' cabins, adhere to Procedures for assisting victims of assault, carry medical supplies, and have at least one crew member trained in crime scene investigation
H.R. 3570	Satellite Home Viewer Update and Reauthorization Act of 2009	Requires satellite carriers and copyright holders to participate in a process to set royalty rates for certain types of transmissions

Table 8. (Continued)

Bill Number (Committee or status)	Title of Legislation	Description of Mandate
		Requires broadcasters and copyright holders to allow satellite providers to retransmit network signals of certain stations without paying royalties
		Increases the royalties that cable carriers pay for retransmitting the signals of distant network stations
		Requires satellite and cable carriers to pay filing fees to the Copyright Office for any royalty payments incurred from retransmitting distant network signals and to allow copyright holders to audit their lists of subscribers
		Limits the ability of copyright owners to collect co-mpensation when secondary transmissions of copy-righted works are made for emergency purposes
		Requires satellite carriers to submit additional information about subscribers
H.R. 3596	Health Insurance Industry Antitrust Enforcement Act of 2009	Imposes a mandate on issuers of health insurance and medical malpractice insurance by partially rep-ealing their exemptions from federal antitrust laws
H.R. 3792	Ryan White HIV/AIDS Treatment Extension Act of 2009	Requires medical facilities to comply with new pro-cedures for notifying emergency response employ-yees of possible exposures to an infectious disease
H.R. 3818	Private Fund Investment Advisers Registration Act of 2009	Requires investment advisers of hedge funds and private equity firms to register with the Securities and Exchange Commission (SEC)
		Requires investment advisers of private funds to maintain records and provide information to the SEC upon request
H.R. 3890	Accountability and Transparency in Rating Agencies Act	Requires nationally recognized statistical rating organizations to comply with several requirements with respect to disclosures, reports, certain polic-ies, employees, and services provided that are unrelated to credit-rating services
		Imposes disclosure requirements on issuers of certain financial products and corporate debt
H.R. 3949	Veterans' Small Business Assistance and Servicemembers Protection Act of 2009	Prohibits telephone, cable, Internet, and residential utility services, as well as lessors of real property and motor vehicles, from imposing early termin-ation fees when service members cancel contracts
S. 38	Professional Boxing Amendments Act of 2009	Requires individuals and organizations in the boxing industry to be licensed by the United States Boxing Commission and to comply with standards for safety, contracts, and reports
		Requires private entities, if subpoenaed, to provide evidence or testimony
S. 69	Commission on Wartime Relocation and	Requires private entities, if subpoenaed, to provide evidence or testimony

Table 8. (Continued)

Bill Number (Committee or status)	Title of Legislation	Description of Mandate
	Internment of Latin Americans of Japanese Descent Act	
S. 139	Data Breach Notification Act	Requires certain businesses to provide notifications in the case of a security breach
S. 212	Gulf of the Farallones and Cordell Bank National Marine Sanctuaries Boundary Modification and Protection Act	Expands the boundaries of the sanctuaries and extends to the expanded area regulations that prohibit certain activities
S. 256	Combat Methamphetamine Enhancement Act of 2009	Requires distributors and retailers of certain mail-order products to submit self-certification documents
		Prohibits anyone from supplying certain mail-order products to a retailer unless the retailer has completed the self-certification or has registered with the Drug Enforcement Agency
S. 275	Children's Health Insurance Program Reauthorization Act of 2009	Requires group health plans to permit employees to enroll in the plan if they lose eligibility for Medicaid or the Children's Health Insurance Program or become eligible through those programs for assistance in paying premiums
		Requires employers to inform employees of potential opportunities for assistance in paying premiums
S. 515	Patent Reform Act of 2009	Requires patent holders and applicants to pay fees
S. 588	Cruise Vessel Security and Safety Act of 2009	Requires certain cruise vessels to meet safety standards, comply with disclosure and recordkeeping requirements, limit the access of crew members to passengers' cabins, adhere to procedures for assisting victims of assault, carry medical supplies, and have at least one crew member trained in crime scene investigation
S. 599	Federal Firefighters Fairness Act of 2009	Requires medical facilities to comply with new procedures for notifying emergency response employees of possible exposures to an infectious disease
S. 728	Veterans' Benefits Enhancement Act of 2009	Requires employers to grant protection of the wages and salaries of service members
S. 850	Shark Conservation Act of 2009	Prohibits the possession, transfer, or landing of shark fins without the carcass naturally attached
S. 1023	Travel Promotion Act of 2009	Requires members of the travel and tourist industry to pay an annual assessment if the Corporation for Travel Promotion is created
S. 1105	Aamodt Litigation Settlement Act	Imposes a mandate if the Secretary of the Interior condemns property to implement the settlement

Table 8. (Continued)

Bill Number (Committee or status)	Title of Legislation	Description of Mandate
S. 1261	Providing for Additional Security in States' Identification Act of 2009	Prohibits storing, reselling, sharing, or trading information obtained by scanning an identification card or tracking the use of such a card
S. 1494	Intelligence authorization Act for Fiscal Year 2010	Requires private entities, if subpoenaed, to provide evidence or testimony
S. 1670	Satellite Television Modernization Act of 2009	Requires satellite carriers and copyright holders to participate in a process to set royalty rates for certain types of transmissions
		Requires broadcasters and copyright holders to allow satellite providers to retransmit network signals of certain stations without paying royalties
		Requires low-power stations to allow satellite carriers to provide secondary transmissions to subscribers within a local market without paying royalties
		Increases the royalties that cable carriers pay for retransmitting the signals of distant network stations
S. 2764	Satellite Television Extension and Localism Act of 2009	Extends an authorization for satellite providers to retransmit distant signals to unserved households without obtaining consent or providing compensation to broadcasters
		Prohibits broadcasters from entering certain exclusive contracts for the rights to retransmit their programs
		Requires satellite carriers that provide local high-definition (HD) channels to also provide HD signals for local noncommercial, educational stations
S. 2768	National Transportation Safety Board Reauthorization Act of 2009	Requires air carriers to make a reasonable attempt to notify the family of each passenger within 60 days before any planned destruction of unclaimed possessions after an accident
S.J. Res. 17	A joint resolution approving renewal of import restrictions contained in the Burmese Freedom and Democracy Act of 2003, and other purposes	Renews the ban on imports from Burma

Source: Congressional Budget Office.

a. In certain cases, proposed legislation reviewed by CBO contained multiple mandates, some of which did not have costs exceeding the statutory threshold.

b. The staff of the Joint Committee on Taxation (JCT) examines legislative provisions that affect the tax code for federal mandates and estimates their costs. Such information is incorporated into CBO's mandate statements.

c. JCT did not determine whether the costs of that mandate would exceed the private-sector threshold established in the Unfunded Mandates Reform Act.

APPENDIX A. AN OVERVIEW OF KEY PROVISIONS IN THE UNFUNDED MANDATES REFORM ACT

The Unfunded Mandates Reform Act of 1995 (UMRA) comprises four titles that address how various parts of the federal government should handle proposed and existing mandates imposed on state, local, and tribal governments and on the private sector.

- Title I, Legislative Accountability and Reform, requires the Congressional Budget Office (CBO) and authorizing committees that oversee federal programs and authorize appropriations to develop and report information about the existence and costs of mandates B in proposed legislation. It also establishes mechanisms for bringing that information to the attention of the Congress before such legislation is considered on the floor of the House or Senate.
- Title II, Regulatory Accountability and Reform, applies to actions of federal agencies in implementing federal law. It requires most agencies in the executive branch (except some independent regulatory agencies) to assess the effects of their regulatory actions on state, B local, and tribal governments and on the private sector. It also requires that statements about such effects accompany certain significant regulations, that agencies seek input from other levels of government in developing regulations, and that agencies consider alternatives that would ease the financial burden of regulations.
- Title III, Review of Federal Mandates, required the now-defunct Advisory Commission on Intergovernmental Relations (ACIR) to prepare three reports: a baseline study of the costs and benefits of federal mandates imposed on state, local, and tribal governments; B a review of the impact of unfunded federal mandates on those governments along with recommendations for easing, consolidating, or terminating mandates; and an annual report identifying federal court rulings that required state, local, or tribal governments to undertake additional responsibilities and activities.[5]
- Title IV, Judicial Review, allows for limited judicial review of certain actions by agencies and of rules developed under title II of UMRA.

This appendix focuses on Title 1, which prescribes CBO's B responsibilities under the act.

Defining Mandates and Their Costs

Under UMRA, a mandate is any provision in legislation, statute, or regulation that would impose an enforceable duty on state, local, or tribal governments or the private sector or that would reduce or eliminate the amount of funding authorized to cover the direct costs of existing mandates. Duties that are imposed as a condition of federal assistance or that arise from participation in a voluntary federal program, such as programs that require entities to have licenses to graze on federal land, are not mandates. Under some large entitlement programs—those that provide $500 million or more annually to state, local, or tribal governments—a new condition on, or a reduction in, federal assistance would be a mandate, but only if those governments lack the flexibility to offset the new costs or the loss of federal funding with reductions elsewhere in the program.

Direct costs are defined in the law as amounts that the private sector or state, local, or tribal governments would be required to spend to comply with the enforceable duty, including amounts that states, localities, or tribes "would be prohibited from raising in revenues." Direct costs exclude amounts that those entities would spend to comply with applicable laws, regulations, or professional standards in effect when the federal mandate is adopted. In addition, direct costs are offset by direct savings that would result from complying with the mandate or by savings from other provisions of the same legislation that govern the same activity as that affected by the mandate.

Because the term "mandate" is defined narrowly in UMRA, the budgetary impacts that legislation imposes on other governments or the private sector are not all the result of such mandates. For example, any costs associated with complying with conditions of receiving grants for most new or existing programs are not considered mandate costs under UMRA. Most of the nonmandate costs for other governments or the private sector that CBO identifies when reviewing bills would result from conditions for receiving federal aid or participating in voluntary federal programs.

The scope of UMRA is further narrowed by the fact that it excludes certain legislative provisions from its procedures. Such provisions include those that deal with constitutional rights, discrimination, emergency aid, accounting and auditing procedures of grants, national security, treaty ratification, and title II of the Social Security Act (Old-Age, Survivors, and Disability Insurance benefits).

Determining what constitutes a mandate under UMRA is not straightforward. Although an activity (such as sponsoring an immigrant's entry into the United States) may be voluntary, the federal program that governs such activity (immigration law) is not. In that instance, a bill imposing new requirements on sponsors of immigrants would constitute a mandate under UMRA. In contrast, other federal programs in which participation is voluntary may impose requirements on their participants that, by UMRA's definition, are not mandates. For example, the National Salvage Motor Vehicle Consumer Protection Act of 1999 (S. 655 in the 105th Congress) contained no intergovernmental mandates, according to CBO. The bill would have imposed additional requirements on states that chose to participate in the National Motor Vehicle Title Information System; it also would have imposed additional costs, including higher annual operating expenses and one-time charges to modify the titles of vehicles and print new forms—which together might have exceeded several million dollars for participating states. Distinctions between what is voluntary in a piece of legislation and what is mandatory are not always clear. However, state, local, and tribal governments may incur significant costs under a proposed law when they participate voluntarily. CBO identifies those costs whenever possible.

In addition, measuring the costs of extending a mandate that is set to expire has, in the past, presented CBO with difficulty in determining whether the statutory thresholds would be exceeded. UMRA is unclear about whether the incremental costs of such an extension should be measured as if the mandate would expire or as if the mandate would continue. That ambiguity has, in previous years, led CBO to report costs using both comparisons. CBO has concluded that the costs of extending a mandate in such cases should be estimated relative to the costs that would be incurred if the mandate were to expire. That method of measuring costs is consistent with the way that certain federal costs are estimated and allows CBO, in cases in which costs can be estimated, to determine whether a mandate's direct cost would exceed the threshold.

CBO's Role in Preparing Mandate Cost Statements

The law requires CBO to give any Congressional authorizing committee that reports a bill a statement about the direct costs of any mandates that CBO identifies in the bill. If the total direct costs of all mandates in the bill are above a specified threshold in any of the first five fiscal years in which the mandate is effective, CBO must provide an estimate of those costs (if feasible) and explain the basis of its estimate. The statutory thresholds are $50 million for intergovernmental mandates and $100 million for private-sector mandates in 1996 dollars, adjusted annually for inflation. (The thresholds in 2009 were $69 million for intergovernmental mandates and $139 million for private-sector mandates.)

The mandate statement that CBO prepares also must include an assessment of whether the bill authorizes or otherwise provides funding to cover the costs of any new federal mandate. In the case of intergovernmental mandates, the cost statement must, under certain circumstances, estimate the appropriations needed to fund such authorizations for up to 10 years after the mandate takes effect.

UMRA also requires committees in the Congress to account for information about the existence and costs of mandates in proposed legislation. Authorizing committees must publish CBO's mandate statements in their reports or in the *Congressional Record* before a bill is considered on the floor of the House or the Senate. Conference committees must, "to the greatest extent practicable," ensure that CBO prepares statements for conference agreements or amended bills if they contain mandates not previously considered by either the House or the Senate or if they impose direct costs that are greater than those in a version considered earlier.

The Congress may also call on CBO to prepare analyses of federal mandates at other stages of the legislative process. At the request of a Senator, CBO must estimate the costs of intergovernmental mandates contained in an amendment the Senator may wish to offer. At the request of the chairman or ranking member of a committee, CBO will help analyze the impact of proposed legislation, conduct special studies of legislative proposals, or compare a federal agency's estimate of the costs of proposed regulations to implement a federal mandate with CBO's estimate.

Enforcement Mechanisms

Section 425 of UMRA sets out rules for both the House and the Senate that prohibit either chamber from considering legislation unless certain conditions are met. Specifically, UMRA prohibits the consideration of a reported bill unless the committee has published a statement from CBO about the costs of any mandates.

The rules preclude consideration for reported legislation that contains intergovernmental mandates with direct costs above the statutory threshold unless the legislation provides direct spending authority or authorizes appropriations sufficient to cover those costs. An authorization of an appropriation will not be sufficient unless the authorized amounts are specified for each year (up to 10 years) after the effective date and the legislation provides a way to terminate or scale back the mandate if the federal agency determines that the appropriated funds are not sufficient to cover those costs.

Finally, although UMRA does not specifically require CBO to analyze the cost of mandates in appropriation bills, it is not in order to consider legislative provisions in such bills—or amendments to them—that increase the direct costs of intergovernmental mandates unless an appropriate CBO statement is provided.

Those rules are not automatically enforced, however; a Member must raise a point of order to enforce them. If a point of order is raised in the House, the full House votes on whether to consider the bill regardless of whether there is a violation. If a point of order is raised in the Senate, the bill may not be considered unless the Senate waives the point of order or it is overturned by the chair or the full Senate.[6]

Appropriation Bills

UMRA does not expressly require CBO to prepare mandate statements for appropriation bills, and CBO has never done so. In general, UMRA's points of order do not apply to the provisions of bills or resolutions reported by the appropriations committees (except legislative provisions), even if those provisions would increase the direct costs of an intergovernmental mandate without providing funding and do not have a mandate statement.[7]

APPENDIX B. Public Laws That Contain Federal Mandates as Defined in the Unfunded Mandates Reform Act, 1996 to 2009

Over the 1996–2009 period, the Congressional Budget Office has identified intergovernmental mandates with costs estimated to exceed the threshold in less than 1 percent of public laws and private-sector mandates with such costs in less than 5 percent of public laws. This appendix lists the intergovernmental (Table B-1) and private-sector (Table B-2 on page 70) mandates enacted since 1996 with estimated costs that exceed the annual thresholds established in the Unfunded Mandates Reform Act.

Table B-1. Intergovernmental Mandates Enacted Whose Estimated Costs Exceed the Statutory Threshold, 1996 to 2009.

In the 14 years since the Unfunded Mandates Reform Act (UMRA) became law, only 11 laws have been enacted that contained intergovernmental mandates with costs above the threshold. In 1996, the threshold for intergovernmental mandates was $50 million. That amount has been adjusted annually for inflation, and in 2009 the threshold was $69 million.

Topic	Description of Mandate	Public Law Number
Child Support	Eliminates matching federal payments for some child support spending. States would be required to use more of their own resources to administer the program, and the Congressional Budget Office (CBO) estimated that additional state spending would total more than $100 million annually, beginning in 2008.	109-171
Driver's Licenses, Identification Cards, and Vital Statistics Documents	Requires state and local governments to meet certain standards for issuing driver's licenses, identification cards, and vital statistics documents. CBO estimated that those governments would spend more than $100 million over the 2005–2009 period to comply and that the costs in at least one of those years would exceed UMRA's threshold. The law authorized the appropriation of funds to provide grants to state and local governm-ents to pay those costs. In fiscal year 2006, $40 million was appropriated for that purpose.	108-458
Food Stamp Administration	Reduces federal funding for administering the Food Stamp program (now the Supplemental Nutrition Assistance Program). CBO estimated the mandate would cost states between $200 million and $300 million a year.	105-185
Internet Taxation	Preempts (temporarily) states' authority to tax certain Internet services and transactions. CBO estimated that the preemption would result in a reduction of at least $300 million in state and local government revenues	108-435
	Extends the preemption contained in Public Law (P.L.) 108-435 of states' authority to tax certain Internet services and transactions through most of 2011. CBO estimated that the extension of the preemption would result in a reduction of about $80 million annually in state and local government revenues	110-108

Table B-1. (Continued)

Topic	Description of Mandate	Public Law Number
Minimum Wage	Increases the minimum wage paid by state and local governments to their employees. CBO estimated the mandate would cost those governments more than $1billion during the first five years that P.L. 104-188 was in effect and slightly less than $1 billion during the first five years that P.L. 110-28 was in effect.	104-188, 110-28
Premium Taxes on Prescription Drug Plans	Preempts state taxes on premiums for certain prescription drug plans. CBO estimated that under the preemption states would lose about $70 million in revenues in 2006 (the first year in which the mandate was in effect). That drop in revenues was estimated to grow to about $95 million in 2010.	108-173
Rail and Transit	Requires all public transit and rail carriers to train workers and submit reports to the Department of Homeland Security. CBO estimated that the cost of the requirements would exceed the threshold in at least one of the first five years following enactment.	110-53
	Requires commuter railroads to install train control technology. CBO estimated that the cost of the requirement would exceed the threshold in at least one of the first five years following enactment.	110-432
Tax Withholding	Requires state and local governments to withhold taxes on certain payments for property and services. The staff of the Joint Committee on Taxation estimated that, beginning in 2011, the cost of the requirement would exceed the intergovernmental threshold established in UMRA.	109-222

Source: Congressional Budget Office.

Table B-2. Private-Sector Mandates Enacted Whose Estimated Costs Exceed the Statutory Threshold, 1996 to 2009.

Less than 5 percent of the public laws enacted since the Unfunded Mandates Reform Act became effective in 1996 have contained private-sector mandates with costs estimated to exceed the threshold. The threshold established in UMRA for private-sector mandates was $100 million. That amount has been adjusted annually for inflation, and in 2009 the threshold was $139 million. Since 1996, 84 private-sector mandates whose costs the Congressional Budget Office determined were higher than the statutory threshold have been enacted. More than 50 percent (46 mandates) involve taxes or fees.

Topic	Description of Mandate	Public Law Number[a]
Agriculture	Changes the method by which minimum prices are established for fluid milk in different regions of the country	106-113

Table B-2. (Continued)

Topic	Description of Mandate	Public Law Number[a]
	Requires country-of-origin labels for various foods	107-171, 110-246
Aviation Security	Imposes security procedures and a user fee to fund aviation security programs	107-71
Bankruptcy	Changes procedures for administering bankruptcy claims	109-8
Campaign Finance Reform	Changes procedures for the collection and use of campaign contributions	107-155
Coal Mines	Imposes mining reclamation fees on operators of coal mines	109-54, 109-234, 109-432
	Requires operators of underground coal mines to install equipment to improve accident preparedness	109-236
Consumer Product Safety	Requires manufacturers, distributors, retailers, and importers of consumer products to abide by new standards and labeling requirements	110-314
Elimination of Right to Seek Compensa-tion Energy	Limits possible recoveries on terrorism-related lawsuits against Libya	110-301
	Requires motor vehicle fuel to contain a certain volume of fuel from a renewable source	109-58, 110-140
	Establishes new energy-efficiency standards for appliances and lighting products	110-140
Finance	Imposes new requirements on credit agencies, lenders, and merchants that handle credit transactions	108-159
	Requires certain depository institutions to pay higher premiums for deposit insura-nce	109-171, 111-22
	Imposes new requirements on issuers of credit card and gift cards	111-24
Government Fees	Requires companies and other entities to pay certain fees when filing a petition for an H-1B visa	108-447
	Imposes fees on holders and applicants of patents and trademarks	108-447, 110-161, 111-8, 111-117, 111-145
	Imposes a surcharge on the filing fee for passport applications	109-167
	Extends customs user fees	110-138, 110-246, 110-436, 111-124
Health Insurance	Requires health insurers to improve portability and continuity of health insurance coverage	104-191
	Requires certain health plans to provide for minimum-length maternity stays	104-204

Table B-2. (Continued)

Topic	Description of Mandate	Public Law Number[a]
	Imposes requirements on private health insurance providers under the Medicare program	105-33
	Requires parity in insurance coverage for mental health and other medical benefits	107-147, 110-343
	Prohibits providers of group health coverage from offering incentives to military retirees to decline enrollment in a group health plan in favor of relying on the military's health care program	109-364
	Modifies requirements and conditions of continued coverage under the Consol-idated Omnibus Budget Reconciliation Act (COBRA) for certain Employyers who offer group health insurance	111-5
Housing	Requires Fannie Mae and Freddie Mac to contribute to a fund for affordable hou-sing programs	110-289
Immigration	Imposes requirements on sponsors of immigrants	104-208
Minimum Wage	Increases the minimum wage paid by employers	104-188, 110-28
Motor Vehicles	Imposes new safety requirements on manufacturers of automobiles	107-318, 110-189
	Expands safety requirements for commercial motor carriers	109-59
	Establishes new standards for corporate average fuel economy (CAFE) standards for motor vehicles	110-140
Pharmaceuticals and Medical Devices	Requires drug manufacturers, at the request of the Food and Drug Adminis-tration, to conduct studies to determine the safety and efficacy of drugs and biological products for use in children and to develop appropriate formulations	108-155
	Extends user fees for manufacturers of prescription drugs and medical devices	110-85
Rail Transportation	Requires rail carriers and bus services to implement security plans and conduct security training	110-53
	Requires railroad carriers to develop and install train control technology	110-432
Retirement	Increases required contributions for retirement	105-33
	Increases certain premiums to be paid to the Pension Benefit Guaranty Corpor-ation by sponsors of single employer and multiemployer defined-benefit pension plans	109-171

Table B-2. (Continued)

Topic	Description of Mandate	Public Law Number[a]
	Shortens the schedule for vesting in private retirement funds	109-280
Revenue-Raising Provisions	Requires individuals or businesses to pay more in taxes	104-188, 104-193, 105-2, 105-34, 105-178, 105-206, 105-277, 106-170, 107-147, 108-357, 109-222 (3 mandates), 110-28, 110-140, 110-343 (6 mandates), 111-3, 111-5, 111-12; 111-69, 111-92 (2 mandates), 111-116
Telecommunications	Requires carriers to provide interconnection and universal service and to block certain programs	104-104
	Prohibits the use of a spectrum by extending the deadline for the transition to digital television	111-4
Tobacco Products	Imposes fees on manufacturers and importers of tobacco products	108-357, 111-31

Source: Congressional Budget Office.

Note: The list of enacted private-sector mandates with costs exceeding the threshold is not necessarily comprehensive for the 1996–2001 period. Each year during that time, CBO analyzed the status of mandates in legislation that it had reviewed during the previous year to determine whether those mandates had been enacted. Some mandates were enacted but were not considered by a committee during the legislative process and thus might not have been reviewed by CBO. To address that issue, CBO in 2002 began to review all public laws enacted each year to determine whether they contained private-sector mandates.

a. Each public law contains one mandate unless noted otherwise.

APPENDIX C. PRIMARY CONTRIBUTORS TO CBO'S ANALYSES OF MANDATES

The following Congressional Budget Office (CBO) staff members prepare the mandate statements that CBO produces for bills and other legislative proposals.

Intergovernmental Mandates

Budget Analysis Division

Leo Lex	Unit Chief, State and Local Government Cost Estimates
Elizabeth Cove Delisle	Commerce, banking, housing, general government
Burke Doherty	Agriculture, education, defense, international affairs
Melissa Merrell	Administration of justice, disaster relief, natural resources, Indian affairs, immigration
Ryan Miller	Energy, environment, general science, space and technology, transportation, water resources
Lisa Ramirez-Branum	Health, human resources, income security, Social Security, training, employment
Ernestine McNeil	Administrative support

Private-Sector Mandates

Microeconomic Studies Division[8]

Patrice Gordon	Unit Chief, Private-Sector Mandates
Amy Petz	Energy, environment, water resources, natural resources, agriculture, Outer Continental Shelf, general science
Paige Piper/Bach	Financial services, governmental affairs, homeland security, intellectual property
Brian Prest	Environment, financial services
Marin Randall	Administration of justice, consumer and occupational health and safety, international affairs, Indian affairs, international trade
Samuel Wice	Transportation, telecommunications, Coast Guard, commerce
Judith Cromwell	Administrative support

Health and Human Resources Division

Nabeel Alsalam	Coordinator, education, income security, and labor
Stuart Hagen	Coordinator, health
David Auerbach	Health
Colin Baker	Health
Patrick Bernhardt	Health, income security
Anna Cook	Health
Noah Meyerson	Labor, income security
Keisuke Nakagawa	Health, income security

Macroeconomic Analysis Division

Kim Kowalewski	Financial services

National Security Division

Elizabeth Bass	Coordinator, Department of Defense and veterans'issues
Daniel Frisk	Defense, veterans' issues
Cynthia Cleveland	Administrative support

Tax Analysis Division

Mark Booth	Unit Chief, Revenue Estimating
Zachary Epstein	Revenues
Grant Driessen	Revenues

Office of the General Counsel

Mark Hadley	General Counsel
T.J. McGrath	Deputy General Counsel

End Notes

[1] UMRA does not define the term "enforceable duty," but the Congressional Budget Office has interpreted it as encompassing actions by public and private entities that would be either required or prohibited.

[2] Authorizing committees have legislative jurisdiction over the establishment, continuation, operations, and authorization of appropriations for federal programs or agencies.

[3] The staff of the Joint Committee on Taxation examines legislative provisions that affect the tax code to identify federal mandates and estimates their costs. CBO's mandate statements incorporate such information.

[4] The intergovernmental and private-sector thresholds established in UMRA were $50 million and $100 million, respectively, in 1996.

[5] ACIR completed and released the report on judicial mandates in July 1995. In January 1996, the commission published a preliminary report on the impact of federal mandates imposed on state and local governments. ACIR received no appropriations after fiscal year 1996 and was terminated at the end of that year.

[6] For more information about points of order, see House Committee on Rules, "The Unfunded Mandate Point of Order," *Parliamentary Outreach Program Newsletter*, vol. 106, no. 11 (June 18, 1999), www.rules.house.gov/Archives/pop106_11.htm.

[7] In many cases, it is not clear what constitutes a legislative provision in an appropriation bill. Therefore, CBO prepares mandate statements for those bills only when requested. On an informal basis, however, CBO reviews all appropriation bills as they move through the legislative process and alerts the appropriation clerks if it identifies any intergovernmental mandates.

[8] Jacob Kuipers, a former CBO staff member, also contributed to CBO's mandate analyses in 2009.

CHAPTER SOURCES

The following chapters have been previously published:

Chapter 1 – This is an edited, reformatted and augmented version of a Congressional Research Service publication, Report R40957, dated December 6, 2010.

Chapter 2 – This is an edited, reformatted and augmented version of a Congressional Budget Office Publication No. 4108, dated March 2010.

INDEX

#

20th century, 16
21st century, 41, 43

A

abuse, 16, 118
access, 44, 82, 87, 92, 97, 98, 99, 100, 103, 112, 119, 121
accountability, 33
accounting, 2, 7, 15, 16, 124
administrators, 85, 114
adverse effects, 12
Advisory Commission on Intergovernmental Relations (ACIR), 7, 52, 123
advocacy, 29, 39, 40
age, 11, 15, 44, 66, 76, 95, 102, 106, 107, 108, 111
Age Discrimination in Employment Act, 44
agencies, 1, 2, 6, 7, 10, 13, 14, 29, 31, 32, 33, 36, 37, 38, 39, 40, 41, 67, 80, 81, 87, 88, 90, 91, 92, 96, 123, 130, 134
agency actions, 3
agriculture, 133
AIDS, 73, 79, 97, 120
air carriers, 82, 84, 102, 112, 115, 118, 122
air quality, 32
airports, 80, 87, 95, 100, 102, 112, 118
American Recovery and Reinvestment Act, 25, 86, 101
American Recovery and Reinvestment Act of 2009, 86
antitrust, 73, 79, 82, 85, 93, 102, 113, 116, 117, 120
appropriations, 15, 18, 21, 22, 23, 50, 56, 123, 126, 127, 134, 135
Appropriations Act, 24, 55, 72, 74, 75, 78, 79, 81, 86
asbestos, 45
assault, 50, 119, 121
assessment, 31, 42, 121, 126
assets, 57, 58, 85, 86, 109, 110, 115, 117
audit, 2, 7, 15, 16, 97, 103, 120, 124
authorities, 100
authority, 4, 11, 13, 14, 15, 18, 27, 31, 33, 39, 42, 75, 80, 83, 84, 87, 88, 90, 104, 117, 126, 128
automobiles, 131
awareness, 46, 47

B

baggage, 9
balanced budget, 49
ban, 50, 79, 122
banking, 133
bankruptcies, 11

bankruptcy, 81, 85, 91, 102, 103, 112, 113, 130
base, 13, 32, 98
benefits, 6, 9, 18, 31, 32, 34, 37, 40, 50, 56, 66, 86, 89, 90, 93, 95, 97, 98, 107, 108, 114, 123, 124, 131
borrowers, 76
boxing, 98, 120
Budget Committee, 48
building code, 84, 90, 100, 112
Bureau of Land Management, 75
Burma, 79, 122
Bush, George W., 37, 53
businesses, vii, 1, 29, 43, 112, 113, 114, 115, 116, 121, 132
buyer, 118

C

cable service, 94
carbon, 80, 81, 82, 84, 87, 88, 90, 104, 105, 112
carbon dioxide, 90, 112
carbon emissions, 81, 87, 88, 90, 104, 105, 112
certification, 84, 116, 121
challenges, 22, 39
Chamber of Commerce, 30, 39, 43
chemical, 72, 76, 78, 80, 81, 84, 86, 91, 92, 114
chemicals, 80, 91, 92, 114
Chief Justice, 53
children, 51, 131
chlorine, 118
cities, 46
citizens, 43, 49, 50
city, 45
civil rights, 16, 44
classes, 8, 39
Clean Air Act, 32
cleanup, 53
Clinton Administration, 44, 46
coal, 84, 87, 88, 90, 104, 105, 112, 130
Coast Guard, 85, 97, 99, 115, 116, 133
collaboration, 38
color, 10
commerce, 103, 117, 133
commercial, 84, 100, 114, 115, 116, 131
common carriers, 118
communities, 57
community, 41, 43, 44, 89
compensation, 71, 84, 109, 110, 111, 113, 115
compliance, 4, 7, 14, 32, 37, 40, 45, 51, 57, 82, 92, 93, 95, 96, 102, 110, 111, 115, 118
compulsion, 4, 8
computer, 119
conference, 19, 20, 21, 23, 27, 28, 51, 67, 70, 71, 74, 126
Conference Report, 62
congress, vii, 2, 3, 5, 6, 7, 11, 14, 15, 16, 17, 19, 20, 22, 23, 26, 27, 28, 29, 32, 34, 37, 38, 39, 41, 42, 45, 46, 47, 48, 49, 50, 51, 52, 53, 54, 55, 56, 57, 58, 59, 60, 61, 62, 65, 66, 67, 68, 70, 72, 74, 123, 125, 126
Congressional Budget Office, v, 1, 3, 16, 20, 39, 56, 60, 65, 66, 69, 70, 71, 74, 79, 80, 81, 82, 85, 87, 101, 122, 123, 127, 128, 129, 132, 134
congressional hearings, 10
consensus, 10
consent, 55, 79, 119, 122
conservation, 82, 86, 116
construction, 40, 100
consulting, 40
consumer protection, 44, 92
consumers, 73, 93, 96, 102
continental, 133
contingency, 87, 100
Conyers, John Jr., 47
cooperation, 4
copyright, 74, 79, 96, 97, 100, 119, 120, 122
coral reefs, 94, 117
corporate average fuel economy, 131

cost, 2, 3, 7, 9, 15, 17, 18, 19, 20, 22, 26, 27, 28, 29, 30, 31, 32, 34, 36, 37, 39, 40, 42, 43, 44, 45, 47, 51, 66, 67, 68, 71, 75, 76, 86, 103, 106, 107, 111, 125, 126, 127, 128, 129
cost effectiveness, 43
covered mandates, 3
creativity, 41
creditors, 76, 81, 82, 85, 86, 92, 102, 107, 110, 111, 113
criminal penalties, 4, 9
current limit, 42
customers, 17, 87, 88, 90, 104, 105, 112
cybersecurity, 84, 100, 116

D

damages, 73, 79, 81, 84, 91, 102, 117, 119
data collection, 112
debtors, 91, 92, 93, 110, 113
decoupling, 13, 14
defamation, 119
deficit, 49
defined-contribution plans, 114
Department of Defense, 25, 74, 79, 134
Department of Education, 38
Department of Energy, 88, 100
Department of Health and Human Services, 58, 83
Department of Homeland Security, 28, 58, 81, 86, 129
Department of Transportation, 24
depository institutions, 76, 82, 92, 96, 102, 130
depreciation, 13
depth, 38
derivatives, 110, 111, 113, 115
destruction, 122
DHS, 58
dichotomy, 8
digital television, 75, 132
direct cost, 1, 3, 14, 17, 18, 21, 22, 30, 33, 50, 56, 66, 124, 125, 126, 127
directives, 17, 43, 45
disability, 15, 66
disaster, 133
disaster relief, 133
disclosure, 72, 75, 89, 90, 91, 92, 93, 94, 98, 101, 102, 112, 117, 119, 120, 121
discrimination, 2, 7, 10, 15, 30, 40, 44, 124
distribution, 65, 77, 94, 95, 118
District of Columbia, 59, 72, 74, 88, 91
domestic violence, 107, 108
draft, 52
drinking water, 81, 92, 119
drugs, 131

E

economic growth, 5
education, 46, 133, 134
election, 117
electricity, 44, 80, 82, 87, 88, 90, 104, 105, 112
emergency, 2, 7, 15, 73, 79, 82, 87, 97, 99, 100, 111, 112, 120, 121, 124
Emergency Economic Stabilization Act, 113
emergency response, 73, 79, 97, 99, 120, 121
emission, 104, 105
employees, 11, 17, 31, 74, 75, 79, 80, 82, 83, 91, 92, 93, 95, 96, 97, 99, 102, 105, 106, 107, 108, 109, 110, 111, 112, 113, 114, 117, 120, 121, 129
employers, 75, 80, 83, 88, 89, 93, 101, 106, 107, 108, 109, 117, 121, 131
employment, 10, 17, 44, 97, 98, 114, 133
energy, 82, 84, 86, 87, 88, 90, 100, 112, 116, 130
energy efficiency, 88, 100
Energy Independence and Security Act, 24
Energy Policy Act of 2005, 24

enforcement, 10, 11, 13, 16, 19, 22, 39, 51, 96, 119
enrollment, 131
environment, 10, 41, 47, 49, 133
environmental protection, 2, 30, 40, 42, 44
Environmental Protection Agency (EPA), 32, 35, 36, 38, 41, 57, 80, 87, 90
environmental regulations, 57
epidemic, 50
equal opportunity, 17
equipment, 82, 84, 100, 111, 116, 130
equity, 110, 111, 120
evidence, 22, 73, 77, 78, 88, 93, 95, 96, 98, 99, 100, 105, 106, 116, 117, 119, 120, 122
examinations, 82, 92, 96, 105
executive branch, 31, 123
Executive Order, 32, 37
expenditures, 9, 32, 33
exporters, 85, 117
exports, 85, 116

F

FAA, 87, 100, 102, 111
factories, 50
Fair Labor Standards Act, 44
fairness, 48
family members, 85, 117
federal agency, 7, 37, 38, 39, 40, 42, 50, 51, 126, 127
federal aid, 10, 124
federal assistance, 2, 7, 9, 15, 32, 37, 42, 44, 66, 124
federal court decisions, 10
federal fiscal sanctions, 4, 9
federal funds, 16, 52, 113
federal government, vii, 3, 4, 5, 11, 31, 38, 39, 41, 42, 43, 48, 49, 50, 65, 89, 97, 98, 107, 108, 123
federal income tax provisions, 10
federal law, 29, 73, 123
federal legislation, vii, 1, 4, 5, 13
federal mandate, vii, 1, 2, 3, 4, 5, 7, 10, 11, 12, 13, 14, 15, 17, 18, 21, 22, 26, 28, 31, 33, 38, 39, 42, 43, 44, 45, 46, 47, 52, 56, 65, 66, 68, 70, 79, 86, 122, 123, 124, 126, 134, 135
Federal Register, 32, 36
federal regulations, 4, 73, 99
federalism, 4, 5, 8, 10, 12, 42, 43, 48, 49
financial, 2, 3, 4, 9, 14, 15, 17, 30, 38, 42, 45, 82, 83, 84, 89, 92, 105, 109, 110, 113, 115, 116, 120, 123, 133
financial institutions, 83, 84, 109, 110, 113, 115
firearms, 50, 77
flexibility, 15, 42, 46, 124
flight, 115
fluid, 129
food, 27, 83, 89, 90, 95, 96, 98, 104, 105, 106, 107, 108, 109
force, 22, 44, 77
foreign affairs, 16
formation, 125
fraud, 16, 106, 107, 108
Fraud Enforcement and Recovery Act, 73, 78
funding, 3, 4, 5, 6, 9, 10, 12, 13, 14, 15, 19, 27, 29, 33, 52, 65, 66, 67, 114, 124, 126, 127, 128
funds, 15, 16, 33, 50, 52, 65, 73, 75, 77, 81, 91, 110, 111, 113, 120, 127, 128, 132

G

General Accounting Office (GAO), 29, 30, 32, 36, 37, 38, 39, 40, 53, 54, 55, 56, 57, 58, 59, 60
governance, 42
government budget, 28
government policy, 9
government revenues, 128

governments, vii, 1, 2, 3, 4, 5, 6, 7, 8, 9, 10, 12, 14, 17, 18, 19, 27, 28, 29, 30, 31, 32, 33, 34, 37, 38, 39, 40, 41, 43, 44, 45, 46, 48, 49, 52, 53, 56, 57, 58, 65, 66, 71, 72, 73, 88, 89, 93, 94, 95, 99, 123, 124, 125, 128, 129, 135
grant programs, 12, 15, 52
grant-in-aid conditions, 10
grants, 9, 10, 12, 14, 15, 29, 49, 124, 128
greenhouse, 80, 82, 84, 87, 88, 90, 104, 105, 112
greenhouse gases, 80
growth, 2, 5, 26, 45, 49
guidelines, 40, 50
gun control, 50

H

hazardous materials, 95
health, 2, 11, 26, 30, 32, 40, 42, 44, 45, 50, 51, 60, 72, 75, 80, 83, 87, 88, 89, 90, 93, 94, 97, 98, 101, 102, 106, 107, 108, 109, 117, 118, 120, 121, 130, 131, 133, 134
Health and Human Services, 58, 83, 95, 104, 108, 109
health care, 26, 42, 80, 83, 89, 90, 98, 108, 131
health information, 72, 75, 83, 93, 101, 102, 106, 107, 108
health insurance, 75, 83, 88, 89, 90, 101, 106, 107, 108, 118, 120, 131
health services, 106, 107
health status, 106, 107
history, 2, 5, 16, 26, 41, 87, 100
HIV, 73, 79, 97, 120
HIV/AIDS, 73, 79, 97, 120
homeland security, 133
host, 12, 50
house, 2, 5, 6, 12, 21, 22, 23, 26, 34, 37, 47, 48, 51, 52, 55, 59, 60, 61, 62, 66, 67, 84, 93, 94, 103, 123, 126, 127, 135
House of Representatives, 5, 6, 12, 48, 66
housing, 81, 91, 92, 96, 133
Housing and Urban Development (HUD), 24, 25, 41, 55
human, 133
human resources, 133
hunting, 118

I

identification, 28, 40, 122, 128
immigrants, 125, 131
immigration, 125, 133
immunity, 82, 102
imports, 79, 85, 116, 122
incidence, 80, 84, 91, 92, 114
income, 10, 13, 14, 74, 83, 86, 108, 109, 133, 134
income tax, 10, 13, 14, 83, 86, 108, 109
Independence, 24
independent regulatory agencies, 2, 7, 32, 39, 42, 123
individuals, 17, 29, 32, 71, 76, 78, 83, 84, 95, 99, 102, 106, 107, 108, 113, 120, 132
industry, 50, 81, 85, 113, 114, 115, 120, 121
inflation, 6, 18, 31, 32, 58, 66, 69, 126, 128, 129
infrastructure, 84, 100, 116
injury, 117
insertion, 48
institutions, 73, 76, 82, 83, 84, 92, 93, 96, 102, 109, 110, 113, 115, 130
intellectual property, 133
interest groups, 28, 38, 39, 40, 43, 45, 47
interest rates, 73, 102
intergovernmental mandates, 2, 3, 4, 5, 6, 7, 8, 9, 10, 12, 14, 15, 18, 19, 20, 21, 26, 27, 29, 30, 31, 33, 34, 43, 44, 45, 50, 66, 68, 69, 70, 71, 73, 80, 87, 95, 99, 100, 125, 126, 127, 128, 135
international affairs, 133
international trade, 133

investment, 85, 109, 110, 111, 114, 115, 120
investments, 81, 84
investors, 71, 76, 81, 84, 91, 93, 102, 103, 117
Iran, 85, 113, 116
Iran Sanctions Act, 85, 113, 116
issues, 7, 33, 47, 49, 62, 134

J

Japan, 93
jurisdiction, 9, 74, 117, 134
justification, 107, 108

L

labeling, 73, 77, 83, 84, 89, 90, 94, 95, 97, 98, 103, 106, 107, 108, 109, 111, 130
Latin America, 99, 117, 121
laws, vii, 11, 12, 16, 40, 44, 47, 50, 53, 56, 65, 66, 67, 68, 69, 71, 72, 73, 74, 80, 81, 86, 88, 89, 90, 91, 92, 93, 94, 95, 96, 97, 98, 99, 100, 117, 118, 120, 124, 127, 128, 129, 132
laws and regulations, vii, 65
lead, 60
leadership, 48
legislation, vii, 1, 2, 3, 4, 5, 6, 7, 10, 11, 12, 13, 14, 15, 16, 17, 18, 19, 21, 23, 27, 30, 31, 33, 42, 46, 47, 48, 49, 50, 56, 65, 66, 67, 68, 70, 71, 74, 80, 82, 101, 122, 123, 124, 125, 126, 132
legislative proposals, 1, 67, 70, 87, 101, 126, 132
lifetime, 106, 107, 108
litigation, 7
loans, 71, 72, 73, 76, 91, 93, 103, 117
lobbying, 43
local government, vii, 1, 2, 4, 5, 6, 7, 8, 9, 10, 11, 12, 13, 14, 26, 27, 28, 29, 30, 32, 33, 38, 39, 40, 42, 43, 44, 45, 46, 47, 48, 49, 52, 53, 56, 58, 72, 88, 89, 99, 128, 129, 135
luggage, 77

M

magnitude, 44, 69
majority, 13, 21, 22, 48, 61
man, 83, 132
management, 117
manipulation, 111
marketing, 73
materials, 95, 119
matter, 32, 49
media, 46, 47
Medicaid, 12, 13, 15, 23, 29, 42, 75, 117, 121
medical, 73, 79, 82, 85, 89, 90, 97, 98, 99, 108, 111, 116, 117, 119, 120, 121, 131
medical reason, 79
Medicare, 24, 131
mental health, 118, 131
mentoring, 84, 115
mentoring program, 84, 115
mercury, 118
methodology, 46
migration, 50
military, 74, 86, 99, 131
minimum price, 129
minimum wage, 22, 26, 27, 129, 131
modifications, 94
moratorium, 13

N

National Defense Authorization Act, 86, 114, 116
National Governors Association (NGA), 13
national origin, 11
national security, 2, 7, 15, 66, 124
natural gas, 44
natural resources, 11, 133

NCS, 54
nursing, 89, 90
nutrition, 83, 89, 90, 97, 98, 106, 107, 108, 109

O

occupational health, 133
Office of Information and Regulatory Affairs (OIRA), 32
Office of Management and Budget, 31, 35, 39, 57, 58, 59, 60
officials, vii, 1, 2, 4, 6, 7, 10, 11, 12, 13, 14, 26, 29, 31, 32, 38, 40, 42, 43, 44, 45, 46, 47, 72, 74, 85, 117
oil, 99, 116
oil spill, 116
Omnibus Appropriations Act,, 25, 72, 75
operations, 12, 77, 111, 134
opportunities, 75, 117, 121
opportunity costs, 30
opt out, 11, 13
ownership, 75, 83
ozone, 32

P

Pakistan, 78, 84, 86, 116
parity, 131
participants, 30, 38, 40, 87, 88, 104, 105, 109, 110, 113, 114, 115, 118, 125
patents, 130
payroll, 97, 98
penalties, 4, 8, 9
pension plans, 131
permit, 31, 75, 88, 96, 100, 117, 119, 121
petroleum, 113
plants, 80, 84, 87, 88, 90, 104, 105, 112
policy, 8, 9, 11, 12, 13, 26, 39, 40, 41, 51, 53, 54
policymakers, 11, 26
pollution, 49
pools, 89, 90
portability, 130
position effect, 54
power plants, 80, 84, 87, 88, 90, 104, 105
preparation, 37
preparedness, 130
preservation, 45
president, vii, 16, 41, 43, 52, 60, 61, 63, 65
President Clinton, 43
press conferences, 46
price manipulation, 111
prime rate, 102
principles, 9, 48
procedural rule, 66
producers, 104, 105, 112
proliferation, 13
proposed regulations, 1, 6, 126
protection, 2, 11, 16, 30, 40, 42, 44, 73, 78, 82, 85, 86, 89, 90, 91, 92, 95, 96, 97, 99, 100, 105, 109, 110, 114, 115, 116, 121
public administration, 57
public awareness, 47
public health, 2, 11, 30, 40, 42
public interest, 29, 30, 38, 39, 40, 43, 45, 47
public officials, 45
public sector, 18
Public Utilities Regulatory Policy Act, 44

Q

qualifications, 87
quality of life, 49, 50
quality standards, 32

R

race, 10
radio, 94, 113
radioactive waste, 85, 113
ratification, 124
real estate, 81, 85, 113
real property, 97, 120

reality, 10
reasoning, 15
recognition, 119
recommendations, 51, 52, 123
recreational, 84, 114, 115
reform, i, iii, v, vii, 1, 3, 4, 15, 16, 20, 23, 26, 33, 34, 36, 42, 46, 47, 48, 51, 52, 53, 54, 55, 56, 57, 58, 59, 60, 61, 62, 65, 69, 70, 71, 73, 74, 77, 80, 83, 84, 86, 87, 91, 92, 93, 95, 99, 101, 103, 107, 109, 110, 113, 117, 121, 122, 123, 127, 128, 129, 130
regulations, vii, 1, 3, 4, 6, 11, 31, 32, 33, 34, 37, 39, 51, 57, 65, 66, 67, 72, 73, 75, 81, 83, 86, 89, 93, 94, 95, 97, 98, 99, 101, 102, 103, 106, 107, 108, 109, 111, 121, 123, 124, 126
regulatory agencies, 2, 7, 32, 39, 42, 87, 88, 123
regulatory controls, 45
regulatory requirements, 31, 32
Rehabilitation Act, 44
reimburse, 89, 97, 98
relief, 5, 11, 46, 47, 48, 133
religion, 10
Republican Party, 48, 61
requirements, vii, 1, 3, 4, 7, 8, 9, 10, 12, 15, 16, 17, 19, 21, 29, 30, 31, 32, 37, 39, 40, 42, 44, 47, 50, 58, 65, 66, 72, 75, 76, 77, 78, 80, 81, 82, 83, 84, 85, 86, 87, 88, 89, 90, 91, 92, 93, 94, 95, 96, 97, 98, 99, 100, 101, 102, 103, 104, 105, 107, 109, 110, 111, 112, 113, 114, 115, 116, 117, 118, 119, 120, 121, 125, 129, 130, 131
researchers, 41
resolution, 17, 21, 79, 122
resources, vii, 11, 12, 33, 48, 65, 128, 133
response, 4, 73, 79, 97, 99, 120, 121
restaurants, 89, 90, 98, 106, 107, 108, 109
restrictions, 8, 13, 44, 56, 79, 104, 105, 112, 118, 122
retail, 87, 88, 89, 90, 98, 104, 105, 106, 107, 108, 109, 112
retirement, 11, 85, 114, 131, 132
retirement age, 11
revenue, 9, 13, 27, 33
rights, 2, 7, 10, 11, 15, 16, 30, 32, 40, 42, 44, 66, 72, 77, 78, 79, 81, 84, 85, 88, 91, 93, 100, 102, 105, 112, 116, 119, 122, 124
risk, 80, 84, 89, 90, 91, 92, 97, 98, 108, 109, 114
risks, 40
royalty, 79, 85, 94, 96, 97, 100, 113, 119, 120, 122
rules, 2, 6, 7, 8, 10, 11, 14, 15, 22, 32, 33, 34, 35, 36, 37, 38, 39, 40, 42, 43, 67, 77, 84, 100, 116, 123, 126, 127, 135

S

safety, 2, 11, 30, 40, 42, 44, 50, 82, 83, 84, 94, 95, 96, 97, 98, 100, 105, 111, 114, 115, 116, 117, 119, 120, 121, 131, 133
sanctions, 4, 8, 9, 85, 108, 109, 113, 116, 117
sanctuaries, 121
savings, 124
school, 44, 57
science, 133
scope, 3, 30, 40, 41, 124
Secretary of the Treasury, 75
securities, 71, 91, 109, 110, 115
security, 2, 7, 15, 58, 66, 72, 78, 80, 81, 82, 84, 86, 91, 92, 95, 99, 103, 104, 109, 110, 112, 114, 115, 118, 119, 121, 124, 130, 131, 133, 134
sellers, 95, 115, 118
senate, 2, 5, 6, 15, 21, 22, 23, 24, 26, 33, 36, 38, 46, 47, 48, 50, 51, 52, 53, 54, 55, 56, 57, 59, 61, 62, 66, 67, 89, 106, 123, 126, 127
service provider, 85, 97, 114
services, 4, 14, 15, 27, 28, 43, 45, 46, 78, 85, 88, 89, 90, 91, 94, 96, 98, 102, 106, 107,

108, 110, 111, 113, 114, 115, 119, 120, 128, 129, 131, 133, 134
settlements, 72
sex, 10
shape, 6
shareholders, 109, 111, 115
signals, 79, 97, 100, 101, 119, 120, 122
small communities, 57
social group, 10, 39, 42
Social Security, 2, 7, 15, 66, 124, 133
society, 32, 49, 50
software, 118
solution, 7, 49
South Dakota, 53
species, 96, 119
spending, 10, 11, 14, 18, 28, 29, 66, 68, 126, 128
Spring, 53, 55
staff members, 132
standardization, 12
state, vii, 1, 3, 4, 5, 6, 7, 8, 9, 10, 11, 12, 13, 14, 15, 17, 18, 19, 26, 27, 28, 29, 30, 31, 32, 33, 34, 37, 38, 39, 40, 41, 42, 43, 44, 45, 46, 47, 48, 52, 53, 56, 58, 65, 66, 71, 72, 73, 74, 80, 81, 84, 86, 87, 88, 89, 90, 91, 92, 93, 94, 95, 96, 97, 98, 99, 100, 106, 107, 112, 117, 118, 123, 124, 125, 128, 129, 135
state laws, 12, 56, 71, 72, 73, 80, 88, 89, 90, 91, 92, 93, 94, 95, 96, 97, 98, 99, 100, 118
statistics, 28, 128
statutes, 6, 12, 38, 44, 85, 113, 116
statutory direct orders, 9, 10, 14
storage, 90, 112
subscribers, 101, 120, 122
subsidy, 8
substance abuse, 118
Superfund, 53
Supreme Court, 52
survivors, 15, 66

T

tanks, 29
tax base, 13
tax cuts, 13
tax policy, 13
taxation, 13
taxes, 9, 13, 27, 28, 29, 46, 74, 76, 77, 86, 95, 99, 118, 129, 132
taxpayers, 50
technical assistance, 31
technology, 28, 80, 82, 129, 131, 133
telecommunications, 133
tenants, 71, 76, 81, 86, 91, 113
terrorism, 80, 84, 91, 92, 114, 130
the private sector, vii, 1, 3, 4, 5, 6, 7, 8, 14, 17, 18, 19, 27, 28, 30, 31, 32, 33, 34, 37, 43, 47, 65, 66, 74, 123, 124
threshold level, 31
Title I, 6, 7, 14, 15, 17, 19, 26, 27, 29, 31, 32, 33, 34, 36, 37, 38, 39, 40, 47, 57, 60, 62, 123, 125
Title II, 6, 7, 14, 31, 32, 33, 34, 36, 37, 38, 39, 40, 60, 62, 123
Title IV, 7, 123
tobacco, 73, 75, 76, 77, 84, 94, 95, 99, 103, 111, 118, 132
total and partial statutory preemptions, 9, 12
toxic waste, 53
trade, 30, 80, 82, 86, 87, 88, 90, 104, 105, 112, 133
trademarks, 130
trade-off, 30
training, 84, 94, 115, 117, 118, 131, 133
transactions, 27, 72, 73, 81, 84, 89, 102, 113, 116, 128, 130
transmission, 84, 88, 100, 103, 105, 112, 116
transport, 95, 96, 104, 117, 119
transportation, 76, 77, 119, 133
transportation security, 119

Transportation Security Administration, 118
Treasury, 24, 41, 55, 75
treatment, 17, 45, 80, 87, 90, 100, 108, 117
tribal officials, 32, 40

U

Unfunded Mandates Reform Act of 1995 (UMRA), vii, 1, 3, 123
uniform, 16, 38, 89, 90
united, 45, 73, 77, 81, 85, 89, 90, 96, 106, 107, 117, 118, 119, 120, 125
United States, 45, 73, 77, 81, 85, 89, 90, 96, 106, 107, 117, 118, 119, 120, 125

V

validation, 46
vehicles, 88, 97, 104, 105, 112, 119, 120, 125, 131
vessels, 84, 95, 97, 99, 114, 115, 116, 118, 119, 121
victims, 119, 121
violence, 50, 107, 108
visions, 113
vote, 5, 6, 21, 22, 51, 52, 55
voting, 22, 47, 50
Voting Rights Act, 17, 93
vulnerability, 72

W

wages, 17, 121
waiver, 13, 78, 84, 116
war, 50
Washington, 35, 45, 46, 52, 53, 54, 55, 56, 57, 58, 59, 60, 61, 62
waste, 16, 45, 51, 85, 113
waste disposal, 45
waste treatment, 45
wastewater, 45
water, 44, 72, 78, 81, 85, 88, 91, 92, 93, 94, 99, 116, 119, 133
water resources, 133
water rights, 72, 78
weakness, 30
weapons, 50
welfare, 50
welfare system, 50
workers, 2, 28, 30, 40, 42, 106, 129
workplace, 50
worldwide, 77
worry, 49